ROLL CALL

THE ABCs OF
SURVIVING & THRIVING
IN TODAY'S SCHOOLS

MARCY CASSIDY, EdD

Advantage | Books

Published by Advantage Books, Charleston, South Carolina.
An imprint of Advantage Media.

ADVANTAGE is a registered trademark, and the Advantage colophon is a trademark of Advantage Media Group, Inc.

Printed in the United States of America.

10 9 8 7 6 5 4 3 2 1

ISBN: 978-1-64225-665-9 (Paperback)
ISBN: 978-1-64225-664-2 (eBook)

Library of Congress Control Number: 2023917752

Cover and layout design by Matthew Morse.
Illustrations by Adaysia Gallaway, Chloe Havens, Juliunna Shinn.

This publication is designed to provide accurate and authoritative information in regard to the subject matter covered. It is sold with the understanding that the publisher is not engaged in rendering legal, accounting, or other professional services. If legal advice or other expert assistance is required, the services of a competent professional person should be sought.

Advantage Books is an imprint of Advantage Media Group. Advantage Media helps busy entrepreneurs, CEOs, and leaders write and publish a book to grow their business and become the authority in their field. Advantage authors comprise an exclusive community of industry professionals, idea-makers, and thought leaders. For more information go to **advantagemedia.com**.

For my mother, grandmother, and great-grandmother,
who were also classroom teachers, and whose life lessons continue
to inspire and guide me both personally and professionally.

And for my father, who taught me the importance of being right
rather than dead right, *and whose sense of humor*
cultivated my humorous outlook on life's challenges.

CONTENTS

INTRODUCTION

ACADEMIC UTOPIA

Students are seated at their desks with the teacher at the helm of the classroom leading instruction. Sounds from the playground seep through the windows, distracting young learners as they eagerly await the bell to ring for their turn on the slides and swings. Bulletin boards are adorned with colorful messages to welcome students to my first classroom.

Yes, all of these would soon be in my grasp, for I was graduating from college with a degree in education and was prepared to create the same academic utopia I enjoyed as a child for a classroom of my very own. My dream to teach was at my fingertips, and for a good portion of my career, my students and I enjoyed a learning environment that was both structured and engaging, both rigorous and fun. My relationships with colleagues, administration, and parents were healthy and robust. However, over the years, the profession of education has evolved to encompass many more skills than I could have ever learned in college classes. Perhaps, a Ninja Warrior Boot Camp should be added to the syllabus.

During my career as a teacher, principal, and superintendent, I have been hit, kicked, spit upon, headbutted, and knocked down by students during outbursts. Running shoes are a necessity because I have chased students both inside and outside of my school and through traffic. I underwent spinal surgery to replace discs damaged from a fall I incurred when an angry child tripped me. Protection orders have been filed on my behalf because of threats made by dangerous students and parents. Other parents have threatened my safety, cursed at me, questioned my "expert skills" on social media, and presented me with a petition to overturn my disciplinary decisions. In case you're wondering, all the students' behaviors were my fault and/ or my staff's, of course! It has become customary and even a societal norm for parents to question our integrity before considering their children's actions—if they ever do. No wonder we often fear dealing with student behavior. Is it worth the fight?

I'll bet you have plenty of stories just like mine. I'll bet further that, like me, you've questioned your career choice. I wrote this book for educators like us—people who care about kids and education, and wonder how to again find joy in our jobs.

That's not easy to do in the current educational climate. Let's take a look at my experiences.

Pajamas are normal attire at the secondary level accompanied by blankets so that the students can be comfortable while they sleep in class. (That's right; it was the norm until I arrived.) When they're not asleep, they make it clear that whatever is happening on Snapchat is far more interesting than our lessons. Students' attention spans have changed dramatically because of video game usage and social media. They need instant gratification as well as physical activity in the classroom. The days of sitting at a desk, listening to the teacher's lecture, are over. Students need to be entertained and involved in lessons, or they find their own way of entertaining themselves and their peers at the teacher's expense.

The bathrooms are an oasis in school buildings. They offer an escape from the classroom and a secluded area to vape, do drugs, or fulfill a TikTok challenge to damage school property by ripping a urinal, sink, or bathroom stall door off the wall or hinges and then post the accomplishment on social media. When educators discipline a student, they must act quickly when contacting the parent or guardian because—guess what—the student will text their version of the story home in Guinness Book record time.

Each day, it's almost as if teachers and administrators have been dropped into a survivor television reality show. The challenges we face test us with unknown obstacles we may not be prepared to handle. There's also our collective fear factor of how we're going to deal with the traumatic events that have become our new normal. Although we may not have to eat live bugs, live naked on a deserted island, or be placed in a glass tank covered with tarantulas, the challenges are real, and we need a new set of skills to survive.

WE ALL HAVE A DOUG OR DEBBIE

Confession. Ten years ago, the demands of the job had me questioning whether I could remain in this noble profession. I felt beaten down and defeated. I even had this nagging, negative voice in my head. You probably have one too. I finally got so sick of it that I named mine Doug, so that I could differentiate his voice from my own. Doug was a real downer. He told me that the job was too taxing, the demands unreasonable, and the work environment toxic. He liked to point out that the students were out of control and that parents never supported me. So persistent was his voice that I contemplated kicking myself off this survivor reality show. However, there was this other voice in my head that kept telling me that yes, I have been kicked and hit, but I have also been hugged and affirmed by so many that I know I am making a difference in the lives of the students I serve, regardless of what Doug says. There are joyous moments among the many obstacles and hurdles in this new normal for educators. Instead of giving up, I told Doug that his days were numbered, and I was going to survive because in the midst of all the chaos, I still found joy in what I did each and every day! Maybe you have a Doug, a Debbie, or an unnamed voice in your own head. If that's what brought you to this book, keep reading.

This book is a fitness plan for you as an educator that includes strategies to boost your skills professionally. The strategies included have worked for me and my staff. Despite some of the scenarios listed previously, I have had very little turnover in my district and former schools due to the conscious efforts made in creating a healthy climate and culture coupled with professional development that is action-packed with effective classroom and behavior strategies to equip all of us to be not only successful in our work but to find joy in it as well.

Let's get in the right mindset for this journey.

FITNESS CHALLENGE

Prior to reading chapter 1, make a current list of everything that brings you joy as an educator. Keep it handy as you read, for I am certain you will add to it. You'll also find a template on my website.

Once your list is complete, you are ready! Let's get fit!

CHAPTER 1

THE FITNESS CHALLENGE IS REAL

Seated in my office is a repeat offender whose habit is to refuse to do his work and consequently disrupt the class during his "free time." I ask, in an exasperated voice, why he is having such struggles in school today, and his reply is, "Well, I just lost my Christmas spirit." It is May.

As an educator, have you lost your Christmas spirit, so to speak? There are a variety of reasons why this may be happening, and it is not your fault. Before we begin the process of getting fit for school, I think it is imperative that we acknowledge why many of us find ourselves feeling as if we are indeed taking part in a reality television challenge that expects us to survive using the skills we know in situations that are unfamiliar, extreme, and emotionally taxing. Although these situations do not involve a speedboat, helicopter, hazmat suit, or spiders, they are atypical and outside our comfort zone or training, thus causing fear, anxiety, trepidation, and burnout.

Educators are underpaid, unappreciated, and disrespected. Let's face it; we knew the financial situation of teaching when we entered the field. We did not expect to park our Lamborghinis in the staff parking lot. Now, there may be some parked in the students' lot, but we understood our financial reality from the start, and we still chose this career. We did not go into education to strike it rich. We went into the field to serve people. We expected low pay, but we did not anticipate the level of student and adult behaviors we would face, the lack of support and appreciation we would endure, and the devaluation of education by our society as a whole. What began as a very respectable job in a service profession has become less valued by society, and educators are taking the brunt of these unfortunate trends.

I recently attended a professional business conference with my husband outside the field of education. I seldom have the opportunity to accompany him because of my unpredictable schedule. Heck, I am not sure I've even had an official lunch break in the past twenty years. This meeting was eye-opening and a wake-up call for me. The people in attendance were happy. They looked and felt invigorated by their work. It almost felt like a family reunion. This was a far cry from many of the recent education conferences I have attended.

Although I garnered good information at my meetings, the atmosphere was heavy. People seemed stressed, and many of the conversations were negative or even toxic. This is what happens when you are overworked, underappreciated, and living at the stress level of a stroke daily. Teachers and educational leaders are expected to assure the health, well-being, and growth of their students, but what about their own survival, health, and happiness?

At the start of a busy day, I am greeting parents in the main office as they drop off their kids. All of a sudden, a parent starts squirming in her leather jacket and moving about the office. I ask if she is all right. She then reaches deep into her sleeve and pulls out a rat by its tail! I stumble and barrel backward, landing on top of the secretary's desk. The parent says, "I have been looking everywhere for you!" It is her pet rat.

Although this rat was not part of a challenge on a survival show, it certainly caught me off guard, and I was unsure about how to react. That's what's happening to us in schools and classrooms. The situations are unusual, extreme, and unique, which makes them more difficult to plan for and react to with the appropriate skill set. Teachers need an entirely new set of strategies to assist and manage the students assigned to their rosters. Many students seated in today's classrooms have experienced trauma in their young lives, which can result in disruptive behaviors, bouts of anger, and even physical aggression. It's not uncommon for teachers to have to evacuate a classroom of children when a student becomes violent, throws furniture and classroom materials, pulls down or climbs to the top of shelving, or threatens to harm the teacher or classmates. Educators themselves are experiencing trauma, both firsthand in their classrooms and secondarily when they hear about the traumatic experiences their students have endured. Our career is taking on an entirely new facade, and these emotional burdens are taking a toll on us.

> *A student, repeating sixth grade for the third year in a row, comes to school with his driver's license. I tell him how impressed I am that he is willing to study for and pass his driver's test since he has not done any of the work I have assigned to him for weeks. I calmly assure him that we will not be building a student parking lot at our elementary school. "Hence, there will be nowhere for you to park your car," I say. Priorities!*

Student apathy and lack of motivation to learn is another frightening current reality in schools. Many secondary teachers and administrators are faced with the student response, "I don't care" on a daily basis.

These students do not like school, are not motivated to do their work, and do not feel any sort of urgency to change their wayward behaviors. Grades and intrinsic motivation seem to be things of the past.

Primary students lose their value for education at the hands of their parents, many of whom don't consider school attendance a priority. By the time the students reach secondary school, these values are ingrained. It's a challenging, vicious cycle.

Wonderfully talented teachers and educational leaders are leaving the profession because of the enormous level of stress they endure day in and day out. Worse yet are the educators who feel defeated and stuck in the profession, just counting down the years to retirement. They are horribly unhappy and have the potential to become toxic to the climate and culture of your school.

Remember the misbehaving child in the anecdote at the start of the chapter who lost his Christmas spirit? He was struggling with the challenges he faced at school. What do we do to help our students solve their problems? We make accommodations for them and provide them with interventions and support. This is exactly what I plan to do for you. In the chapters to follow, I will provide you with practical solutions to this new current reality in schools. You will be fortified with the tools you need to overcome the obstacles and survive the challenge! It's time to retrofit you with the necessary strategies to revitalize your health, happiness, and professional prowess in your chosen profession. We deserve to be happy too!

FITNESS ASSESSMENT

When you sign up at a new gym or fitness program, one of the first things they do is assess your current physical state. We are going to do that here. Let's check and see how fit you are regarding education, either as a teacher or as an educational leader. Once we have the results, we can delve into the fitness regimen that is going to retrofit you for today's classrooms and schools!

Reflect on the following questions to assess your fitness level (Yes/No Responses):

- When you awake in the morning, you feel excitement and enthusiasm about going to work.
- You enjoy healthy relationships with students, parents, and colleagues.
- You enjoy professional development days and learning new instructional strategies.
- You often integrate new strategies into your lesson plans.
- Your classroom management style is proactive and positive rather than reactive and punitive.
- Your core values are aligned with the core values of the school and district where you work.
- You take care of your emotional health and allow yourself quiet time to meditate, breathe, or unwind.
- You take time for yourself for personal activities that bring you joy.
- You feel appreciated at your school/district.
- Your school or district celebrates successes.
- When confronted with toxic colleagues, you refrain from joining the conversation.
- The climate at your school is happy and healthy.

- You teach a formal social-emotional curriculum to your students.
- You find joy and satisfaction from your work as an educator.

If you answered, "NO" to the majority of the survey questions, then this is the book for you! Your dream may have faded, but your passion has not. Let's get to work.

CHAPTER 2

THE RIGHT FIT

The girls' basketball coach comes to me the morning following a big game. He tells me that prior to the start of the game, a referee warned him that one of our players did not have appropriate shoes and would be excluded from play. Upon investigation, the young woman was wearing light-up wheelies! Although this idea is outside of the box, the coach and I agree with its creativity and that it could potentially change the dynamics of girls' basketball!

You know the feeling we all get when we decide it's time to get back into shape? That feeling of excitement mixed with trepidation. We purchase new shoes and a trendy fitness outfit. We assume we are going to strut right back into the gym with the vim and vigor we once had as younger versions of ourselves. After months of idleness, we arrive at the gym, stretch, and begin the workout. Suddenly, we are gasping for air, feeling as if we are going to be sick, and finding ourselves stunned by the younger athletes running circles around us! To make matters worse, we can barely get out of bed the next day. Our muscles are screaming at us, making it difficult to climb a flight of stairs or get out of a chair without wincing. This is how we are feeling with the current expectations in our schools and classrooms. Our fitness level does not meet the demands of the job. It is time to find the right fitness plan and get back into shape professionally.

We are out of shape and desperately in need of the right gear to survive in today's schools, perhaps not light-up wheelies but definitely the means to propel us to greater professional fitness levels. Although this effort can be as daunting as embarking on a new physical fitness regimen, it also can be inspiring and healing. You are on the path to a new you, a you who is happier, healthier, and energized to be in your classroom or school. Where do we start? We start with the School Improvement Plan.

The hallways of my elementary school are filled with anxious parents and students waiting for Kindergarten Round-Up to commence. The students are divided into groups and dispersed to classrooms. Each teacher has a special activity planned, and the students are to rotate from class to class. In one of the classrooms, the teacher begins to read a book aloud when all of a sudden, a child cries out in a loud voice, "BORING!"

SCHOOL IMPROVEMENT PLAN

Work revolving around the school improvement process can be boring if you allow it to be! Schools and school districts all implement some sort of a School Improvement Plan and a Strategic Plan at the district level that provides a guide for the district's priorities. So often, this sort of work is seen as unpleasant, tedious, and a hoop to jump through to satisfy requirements outlined by the State Departments of Education. Often, a school's leadership team will write this plan in isolation and present the staff with a polished copy that will adorn shelves, collecting dust in classrooms. During my career in numerous districts, I can say assuredly that I have worked with colleagues who never knew the contents of a current School Improvement Plan, so how do we make this process more meaningful to all stakeholders? Involve them, *all of them*, and make the process personal and meaningful.

One way to involve all staff in the school improvement process is to assure that they are familiarized with and a key player in the process. I can hear you groaning right now. You've done this before and believe that there is no way to make this information interesting and engaging! Yes, there is!

Here are a few of the ways I facilitate this process.

1. Teach the Plan: The School Improvement Plan is a live document that should be updated at least annually, but waiting to update the plan just prior to your accreditation visit will render it useless because you are not using it to guide instruction and interventions. I send out weekly announcements that include a section from the plan that asks the staff to review, update, and provide feedback. All staff members are familiar with the plan because it has been broken down for them into manageable pieces and taught to them, and they have the opportunity to provide feedback for changes and improvement to administration.

2. Walk-Through Observations: I tie my walk-through observations to a section of the School Improvement Plan that is sent to the staff Monday morning of each week. I provide positive written feedback (email or a handwritten note) to staff I observe using the strategy highlighted from the plan.

3. Staff Meetings: You simply must meet with your staff once a week, or at a minimum, bi-weekly. Teaching is an isolating profession. We need to come together as a team to discuss the state of the nation, so to speak. These meetings provide time to review a plan. The agenda should not include daily announcements that can be communicated via email. These meetings are to discuss school improvement, period. This is also a wonderful time to celebrate successes. Share examples of teachers using strategies from the improvement plan with the staff. Have teachers share ideas with one another during these meetings as well.

4. Elective Teachers: Oftentimes, elective teachers feel as if they are not connected to the School Improvement Plan because

they do not teach core classes or a subject that is formally tested. I will never forget how, during my first year as a principal, an elective teacher opted to read the newspaper rather than follow along with the School Improvement planning. This is what she was used to doing, and she hadn't ever been formally invited to participate. As you can imagine, I issued her an invitation! I provide my elective teachers with my weekly topic regarding the plan in advance. They then have time to think about how to integrate the standard into their lessons. I ask them to send ideas to the general education teachers of how to integrate art, movement, music, and acting into their lesson plans. Some of my elective teachers have created their own weekly newsletters filled with such ideas.

5. Early Release or Late Start: Teachers never have enough time to plan with one another or take part in a regular regimen of professional development. If possible, provide teachers with early release time or late starts for a period of at least one hour weekly. More than an hour inconveniences your community, and less than an hour does not provide adequate time for effective planning or professional development. These release times should be the same time and day each week to avoid confusion with the community.

6. Strategy of the Week: Along with reviewing a section of the plan weekly, I also provide a mini professional development tip in my weekly newsletter. Typically, I select a strategy that is directly related to our plan in an effort to support teachers. This can be a video, a podcast, a professional article, or part of a book study we are doing as a staff. I then look for teachers using the identified strategy when I am conducting observations and recognize and celebrate them publicly.

DATA

Data is a four-letter word, and it is most likely the most important word you will find in this book. Yes, data can be boring if you allow it to be; however, all our decisions must be based on solid data so that we can move the needle in the correct direction as a staff and school district. I have gathered teams around the meeting table over the years and have witnessed decisions being made without any data. I call this decision-making based on our gut feelings, and it is seldom, if ever, accurate.

1. Present data in small pieces rather than presenting all the district data at one sitting during a professional development day. I don't have to tell you that doing so will make the work unmanageable, overwhelming, and intimidating. Glazed eyes, anyone? Because of its statistical nature, data can be scary to many people. You want your staff to know the numbers, interpret them, and design interventions for improvement, so present that data in user-friendly templates and in small chunks to ease trepidation.

2. Data Digs: Add data to the weekly announcements, and challenge the staff to identify strengths and weaknesses. Ask each staff member to respond to the announcement with one observation about the data and one intervention idea. Compile and share responses. Providing a prize to the staff member who responds first can add an element of fun to working with data.

3. Data Scavenger Hunts: Provide staff with questions they have to respond to after reviewing the data. Offer prizes to staff members who complete the exercise first. Popular options include gift cards, sodas, school supplies, candy, or certificates to leave early or dress down for a day.

4. Data Walls, Notebooks, or Slideshows: Get creative with ways to monitor and track student progress. Offer professional development and support in how to monitor and track student data.

5. Data Software: I highly recommend the purchase of data software. Although some teachers may be intimidated at first, they will soon learn how efficient software makes this process. It also aggregates the data into visual graphs and charts instantly, thus providing all users with clearly organized and uniform data reports. Many options for data software are free.

6. Data Goal Setting: Teachers' professional goals should be aligned with the school's data. Provide a goal template for all staff to utilize. I prefer to use the SMART goal prototype. A student version is available, so staff and students alike can create goals using a common format. Students of all ages have the capacity to monitor and track their own growth and should be creating goals with the guidance of their teachers.

SMART GOAL:

S Specific: What exactly do you want to accomplish?

M Measurable: How are you going to track your progress?

A Achievable: Is the goal challenging yet achievable?

R Relevant: Does this goal align with the School Improvement Plan?

T Time Sensitive: When will you complete this goal? [1]

It is critical that each staff member write goals every school year, both personal and professional goals. Oftentimes,

---

school districts only require teachers to write professional goals if they are being evaluated, giving all others the year off from goal writing, sometimes more than one year if they are evaluated every third year. Know this: Goals inspire people. Goal writing gives us an opportunity to reflect on areas of strength and areas in which we would like to grow.

7. Data Blame Game: One reason teachers fear working with data is that when it is poor, they are embarrassed and self-conscious about the scores their students earned. The climate I cultivate as it relates to data is that the entire school district is responsible for student data. Working with data is not about shaming teachers for their poor performance. It is about identifying where we need improvement and planning appropriate interventions and celebrating successes as a team. However, I will have conversations with individuals if I fear teacher performance is a part of the problem. Is the data compromised because of curriculum or a poor choice in instructional strategies? Is classroom management a concern, and if so, how can I help?

8. Data Celebrations: Do not wait until the end of the school year to celebrate growth and accomplishments. I celebrate such accomplishments at a weekly assembly every Friday morning. The entire school meets in the gym prior to the start of the day for a fifteen-minute assembly, where I ask students and teachers to strut their stuff and be recognized for their efforts and accomplishments. I have them select a Walk-Up song to make the experience that much more personal and fun. If an all-school meeting each week sounds daunting, start with grade-level meetings, but celebrate the wins regularly; it is motivating as well as a great way to keep all parties accountable for the

school or district's data. Classroom teachers can also hold mini celebrations for student successes. You are creating a culture that is data driven and focused on growth. It is critical to celebrate ALL students who have moved the needle on their data and made growth, not just the high-achieving students. In doing so, you will motivate learners of all levels and build their self-esteem as it relates to learning.

9. Flag the Standards: Teachers must know what is to be assessed and where those standards or indicators are taught in their instructional manuals. I have teachers go through their teaching manuals and flag tested standards with blue tabs. Then, they go back

> **Teach the stuff not the fluff.**
> **—Dr. Anita Archer**

through and flag the indicators that will be tested the following year with green tabs. We use yellow tabs to flag indicators taught two years later. Finally, we highlight the indicators that are never tested with pink flags. Once this is done, teachers know exactly what to teach and where those lessons are located in their manuals. They also know what does *not* need to be taught, which saves instructional time for pertinent curriculum. At a minimum, flag the standards that are to be taught (the blue flags) if this process sounds daunting.

Data isn't a four-letter word when it is a natural part of a routine. It also becomes less intimidating, thus making the school improvement process a daily activity rather than an isolated lesson during professional development.

Teach the stuff not the fluff.—Dr. Anita Archer

CORE VALUES

Now, it's time to get personal with the School Improvement Plan. A fun way to motivate staff buy-in regarding the process is to connect it to their beliefs and values. At the start of each school year, I have my staff take part in an exercise that has them identify their core values. I use a list of fifty core values from the work of James Clear, The LeaderShape Institute. We present individuals with a list of fifty words that represent core values, and they have to select the five words that most reflect their beliefs. Responses are then aggregated, and the staff's core values are identified. By doing this exercise, you are sending the message to your staff that you desire and value their input and who they are as individuals. It is not only a fun exercise but telling as well, because participants are able to decide if their core values match those of the school or district as a whole. I also have my secondary students and community members take part in this exercise to assure that, as a district leader, I'm aligning the work I do with the values of those I serve.

I am a superintendent of a small, rural school district. Much of my previous experience has been in urban or suburban settings. On a typical weekday, I am conducting observations in classrooms when a teacher pulls me to the side and says that a student in her class is causing a disruption by making noises with his retainer. I visit with the student, have him put the "retainer" in its case, and tell him he can pick it up at the office at the end of the day. When I drop it off at the office, the secretary informs me that this object is not a retainer but rather a turkey call! This city girl has never seen a turkey call.

Am I the right fit? When the data regarding the work around core values is identified, you have the opportunity to assess if your core values are aligned with the values of your school or district. If not, you must ask if this district is the best fit for you. If you are working for a school district that does not share your core values, this may be the source for your turmoil and unhappiness. For example, I once led a school where I initiated a positive and proactive approach to dealing with student discipline. A handful of teachers simply did not buy into this approach and were constantly at odds with colleagues and me, fighting the system, thus creating a toxic work environment. I pushed forward with this initiative because it aligned with what the majority of my patrons valued, and the teachers who could not embrace this model made the decision to work elsewhere. You must have the courage to leave a position if your core values are compromised. There are other schools with differing approaches. Find a school that shares your professional beliefs and values, and you'll be making the first step to being fit to survive in this profession!

A junior high student approaches me in the hallway and asks, "What kind of video games do you like to play when you get home at night?" I answer, "I actually prefer to read books than to play video games." His response: "That's weird," and he walks off into the sunset.

We all have different interests and activities that bring us joy, even if it means we are weird. In order to inspire teachers and administrators to buy into the school improvement process and create goals for growth, you have to connect their personal interests and values to the process. They then understand that their success is directly related to the success of the school and school district; they have a stake in the game. One way to do this is through the use of vision boards.

VISION BOARDS

The vision board that best complements the school improvement process has a focus on professional and personal goals. Goals, such as winning the lottery, owning a Maserati, or living in a mansion, are not a part of this process. I ask my staff to focus on goals that will propel them forward as an educator and a person.

You are the author of your future! When teachers ask young children what they want to be when they grow up, they respond with adventurous examples, such as an astronaut or a professional athlete. They chase their interests and follow their dreams! Once we become adults, we often put our dreams on the back burner and become complacent in our day-to-day routines, which can cause boredom and burnout. Revitalizing some of those childhood dreams through annual goals and the creation of a vision board helps us remember what brought us into the field of education in the first place. It can also reignite the fire and passion we need to be successful educators today.

You will need professional development time to introduce and begin the development of individual vision boards with your staff. Teachers can opt to create either a digital or a physical vision board.

Steps to creating a vision board:

1. Have employees complete a variety of reflection exercises to begin the process of identifying what is important to them and how each wishes to grow as a person and as an educator.
2. List ideas, topics, or subjects they wish to explore.
3. Define goals.
4. Write action steps, including timelines, necessary to accomplish said goals.
5. Search for pictures, quotes, affirmations, and phrases that can be visual representations of your goals on a vision board.
6. Map out and create your vision board.
7. Come together to share and update vision boards and celebrate goal completion.

Creating a vision board may take more than one professional development session. I host monthly vision board-building parties where I provide treats and materials to staff for their use. We also take time during these sessions to share our boards, ideas, and progress made on our goals. Educators rarely have the opportunity to come together and get to know one another. Vision board building is a wonderful way to interact with a shared purpose. Once teachers have created their vision boards, extend this strategy to students and school-wide goals with a common bulletin board dedicated to school improvement. Individual vision boards should be hung in your line of vision as an ongoing reminder of what one wishes to accomplish. Take a picture of your vision board, and make it the screensaver on your computer and phone. Keep your goals in front of you at all times. To take this process a step further, take pictures of student and staff vision boards and have them scrolling on prompters at school.

Bringing the School Improvement Plan to life through purposeful interactions coupled with a deep understanding of student data and exactly what needs to be taught creates a sense of security for all staff, thus alleviating anxiety. Everyone is speaking the same language, and the ship is moving in one direction. You have also tied the school improvement process to individuals' personal dreams, hopes, and goals, thus making the process more meaningful to all stakeholders. They are well prepared. They know the rules of the game, and they are far more likely to be professionally *fit* for the challenge, even if it includes light-up wheelies on a junior high school basketball court!

COMPREHENSIVE, INTEGRATED, THREE-TIERED MODEL OF PREVENTION

Do you hear the trumpets sounding or the scoreboard blaring? If so, that is because I am about to introduce you to the framework that took the school improvement process for my school district and catapulted it into a highly successful, multitiered approach that addresses more than just the academic needs of our students. As it turns out, you can have the best curriculum ever written along with a clear mission, vision, values, and goals, but there must also be a dedicated focus around students' behavior, character, and social-emotional skills, or the system will fall short, especially since the pandemic. Educators are seeing much higher percentages of students who struggle with significant behavioral and emotional deficits, and such deficits must be met with strategic strategies. Schools no longer own only the academic success of their students. They own the success of the whole child, which includes academics, behavior, and social-emotional skills. Without direct instruction in these areas, students' academic prowess will fall prey to their emotional needs, thus resulting in a decline in test data. Hence, teachers feel defeated as academic data plummets while drowning in an increase in student behaviors. This is the perfect recipe for burnout, and due to such levels of stress, teachers may be tempted to leave the profession as if their hair is on fire. Help is at your fingertips thanks to an effort originated at the University of Kansas—Rock Chalk Jayhawks!

A child runs into my office and scuffles underneath my desk. This is not an unusual occurrence. This youngster struggles to regulate her emotions because of the trauma she has experienced. Escaping the demands of the classroom and hiding under the principal's desk provide her a safe space in which to calm herself. I acknowledge her and let her know I am here if she needs me. Meanwhile, a parent, new to my school, stops in my doorway with her young child. She offers me a cupcake in celebration of her child's birthday. Before I have a chance to respond, the child underneath my desk pops her head up and says, "Cupcakes. I love cupcakes!" The parent in my doorway has a look of horror on her face. My response is, "That's where I keep the naughty children."

Thirty years ago, I would never have imagined that a typical day as a school administrator would involve a child calming herself underneath my desk. Yet, thirty years ago, there was only one focus for educators: academics. This is no longer the case.

It's morning drop-off, or rush hour, as educators like to call it. I am welcoming students when a commotion of honking and hollering ensues. I make my way down the sidewalk to identify the problem and find one of the parents and her three children riding a lawn mower. Her car would not start. Maybe we need to consider two lanes of traffic to accommodate slow-moving vehicles?

Today's schools and classrooms require us to expand our thinking. We no longer have just one lane of traffic or just the academic health of our students to consider. In order to increase our fitness level in the classroom and administrative roles, we must also examine the behavioral, social, and emotional health of our students alongside their academic prowess, thus expanding our highway of knowledge into fast-moving, multifaceted structures.

A few years ago, a salesperson, without making an appointment, was waiting in the lobby of my school to visit with me. So annoying. When I finally had a few seconds to breathe, I motioned him into my office. He looked me in the eye and said, "This place is a circus. Why are so many kids in trouble?" For once, an uninvited salesperson had something notable to say. His words resonated with me, and I realized he was right. We had a handle on the academic aspect of our jobs, but our students were suffering with behavioral and social-emotional skill deficits, and we had no formal plan to address these needs.

I went directly to my leadership team with a plea for help, but when I looked around the table, I realized these teachers looked as tired as I felt. In fact, they were the same teachers sending their students to the office for disciplinary action. We all needed help.

When you campaign for a leadership team, invite the most qualified and forward-thinking staff members to put their names on the ballot.

These are the people who are going to assist you in turning your school around and creating a culture and climate that sustain staff.

I had an amazing leadership team at this time, and after a great deal of research, we found a systemic process for our school that we thought had great promise. The reason this system appealed to us was that it addressed the whole child: Academics, Social-Emotional Skills, and Behavior, a formula to provide real solutions for real problems.

The name of this plan is the Comprehensive, Integrated, Three-Tiered Model of Prevention, or Ci3T.[2] The title of this plan can feel a bit daunting if you let it, but don't give into that temptation. The tenets of this system not only provided my staff with the strategies they needed to address the current needs of our students, but it also shifted our focus from a reactive system to one that was preventive and proactive. Once implemented, the students not only showed significant changes in their overall health, but the health of my staff was on the mend as well.

The benefits of Ci3T are too powerful to ignore and are supported with a wealth of meta-analyses and solid research, and speaking from a practical standpoint, Ci3T has been the most impactful framework I have ever implemented for both staff and students.

Benefits of Ci3T:

- Increases academic performance
- Increases attendance
- Improves emotional well-being and social behavior
- Reduces the number of behavioral disruptions
- Reduces bullying behaviors
- Reduces teacher attrition

---

2   Kathleen L. Lane, "Ci3t.org." *Ci3t.org*, March 12, 2021, ci3t.org.

Nestled in the heart of the country is the University of Kansas, where Dr. Kathleen Lane and her team of educators have created a systemic approach to working with school districts to address the needs of the whole child. Dr. Lane is a distinguished professor at the university in the Department of Special Education. As a remarkable educator, she has dedicated her career to modernizing schools to meet the new demands of students with low-intensity strategies that are practical and easy to implement.

Dr. Lane is highly intelligent, is extremely driven, has been recognized with many honors, and is an accomplished writer. She is a rock star in education, and I may be her biggest fan! However, she remains humble and extremely hands-on in the work that she does with Ci3T and the school districts she serves. The training is free of charge. Dr. Lane's work is funded through a grant. She has created a website, ci3t.org, where all the training materials and information are clearly organized and free to access. Reading lists are provided along with templates for every step of the Ci3T process. Videos for professional development are also included on this website so that all members of your faculty can "meet" Dr. Lane and her team. I have been blessed to work with Dr. Lane and her team for over a decade, and the work she has done has had a greater impact on me and my staff than any other educational initiative in my career. Are you ready to learn more? I hope so, because your professional life is about to change.

CI3T DEFINED

> A mother of one of my students calls the office to inform us that she has just delivered twins! Later that day, I congratulate one of the siblings; there are several in my school and a few more in other schools, for becoming a BIG brother. I ask him for the names of the new babies, and he replies in a very unimpressed manner, "Peanut Butter and Jelly."

This child has given up on remembering all the names of his siblings. It's just too much for him. Educators are faced with more problems today than ever before, and these problems stem from a shift in the needs of today's students from simply academic needs to strategies to manage extreme behaviors and social-emotional deficits. It all can feel very overwhelming, just like a young child struggling to remember the names of multiple siblings. Adding more to our plates and more to remember is not the answer. Organizing our efforts into a purposeful framework is the answer, and that framework is Ci3T.

Ci3T refers to a continuous improvement model of prevention that includes three tiers of support for students so that they can experience success academically, behaviorally (positive behavior interventions and support, PBIS), and socially (e.g., Second Step). Using problem solving and data-based decision-making, this model addresses students' varied needs and offers school leadership teams a structure to consider multiple needs simultaneously in an integrated fashion.

THE CI3T MISSION STATEMENT

Ci3T models of prevention assist schools in creating a comprehensive systems-oriented approach to (a) integrate efforts to support the academic, behavioral, and social competencies of all students; (b) promote collaboration and teaming between all school and community stakeholders; and (c) support educators' efficacy and well-being through data-informed professional learning, clear expectations for staff and students, and supportive, positive environments.[3]

Ci3T provides educators with a framework. It addresses three domains of students' needs as it relates to both remediation and enrichment: academic, behavioral, and social-emotional. The first step in adopting this system is to create your school's blueprint that will document all available strategies and resources your school or district has to address the needs of the whole child. When I rolled out Ci3T, some staff were worried that I was putting more on their plates. This is not true. We deal with students' academic, behavioral, and social-emotional needs every day. Ci3T is a framework for a system

---

3   Kathleen L. Lane, "Ci3t.org." *Ci3t.org*, March 12, 2021, ci3t.org.

to strategically meet these needs in a proactive manner with evidence-based strategies. Spinning our wheels with the reactive system we had in place prior to Ci3T was not working and was, in fact, burning us out and potentially causing some to leave the profession.

Let's begin with a visual:

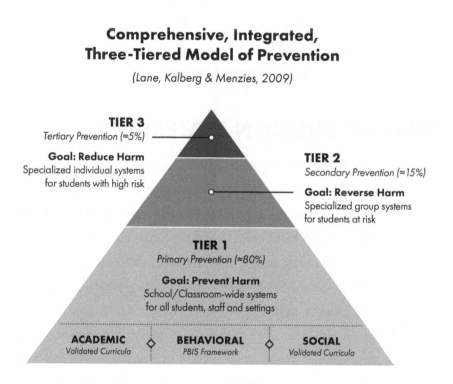

Comprehensive, Integrated, Three-Tiered Model of Prevention

(Lane, Kalberg & Menzies, 2009)

TIER 3
Tertiary Prevention (≈5%)

Goal: Reduce Harm
Specialized individual systems
for students with high risk

TIER 2
Secondary Prevention (≈15%)

Goal: Reverse Harm
Specialized group systems
for students at risk

TIER 1
Primary Prevention (≈80%)

Goal: Prevent Harm
School/Classroom-wide systems
for all students, staff and settings

| **ACADEMIC** | **BEHAVIORAL** | **SOCIAL** |
| *Validated Curricula* | *PBIS Framework* | *Validated Curricula* |

The Ci3T model focuses on three student domains but is also a three-tiered approach to prevention within these domains. Although all students will have access to a viable curriculum and instructional strategies offered in all three areas (academic, behavioral, and social-emotional), approximately 80 percent, on average, will perform proficiently when exposed to said curriculum and strategies. These students fall into Tier One of the Ci3T model. They are responding positively to the universal programs being offered. Benchmarking the students three times a year in all three areas teases out which students fall into this first tier. These are the students who are able to thrive from the instruction and interventions available to everyone, the universal plan. Once benchmarked, some students will demonstrate the need for Tier Two interventions, which are low-intensity (Secondary Interventions) intended to support them, usually around 15 percent of the population. Finally, some students fall into Tier Three (Tertiary Interventions) level of need regarding interventions that involve more intensive strategies designed specifically for them. Students needing Tier Two or even Tier Three interventions are not necessarily in need of special education, but this could be the case should a child continue to underperform for an extended period of time after many interventions have been implemented and failed. Dr. Lane always notes that Ci3T is not about programs but about the people implementing the programs. All teachers serve every child whether or not they have been identified for special education.

CREATING YOUR BLUEPRINT AND IMPLEMENTATION MANUAL

The templates for the Blueprint and Implementation Manuals are located on the website ci3t.org and are very easy to use. As you begin writing these plans, you will need to add your school's Mission and Vision or Purpose statement that has already been completed during the school improvement process. My team morphed the Ci3T Blueprint and Implementation Manual into our School Improvement Plan because Ci3T addresses the whole child unlike any previous plan we had written. Let me be clear. You are not starting over. You already have a plan, and now you are updating it with a research-based, mutifaceted, data-driven framework.

Again, there are three main domains to address (academic, behavioral, and social-emotional) as well as three tiers of instruction and intervention (Tier One, Primary Prevention; Tier Two, Secondary Prevention; and Tier Three, Tertiary Prevention). Students must be assessed at least three times annually in all three domains to identify who is and who is not responding to the universal plan. Interventions are then designed for remediation or enrichment. Ci3T utilizes a data-driven approach to identify and monitor the needs of all students to prevent deficiencies and to respond efficiently and effectively to students' needs.

Transition to the academic domain.

FITNESS CHALLENGE

- What are your core values?
- Are you the right fit?
- Create a vision board.

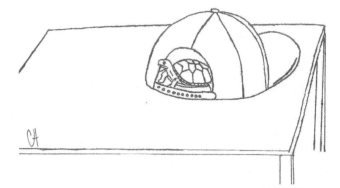

I am teaching a math lesson in a fourth-grade classroom. I thank a student for not wearing his ball cap and let him know I appreciate the fact that he has it placed neatly on the side of his desk. As I continue to teach, I sense that the ball cap is moving on its own. I walk over to the student's desk, pick up the cap, and discover a turtle inhabiting this space. After the initial shock, we walk the turtle outdoors and return it to its natural habitat. This is not on my lesson plan!

The focus of our next chapter is academics. What strategies can you utilize in your lesson plans to prevent students from being on their phones, sleeping, or entertaining animals they might have under a ball cap on their desk? Turn the page for amazing ideas!

CHAPTER 3

THE ABCs OF SURVIVAL

THE **A**CADEMIC DOMAIN

As a new superintendent, I make a visit to the elementary school in an effort to be visible and get to know students and staff. I check in at the main office, where I find a student seated at a cubby next to the secretary. He is obviously in trouble. I introduce myself and inquire as to why he's in the office. He informs me that his teacher assigned a four-page essay and asserts that he completed this assignment and does not understand what the problem is. I ask to see his essay and immediately note that I cannot read a single word. I give the young man the "Teacher" look, and he says, "I wrote it in my own language. I am not sure why my teacher is mad. I provided her with the key." Written in large letters, and in red ink are the words, "REWRITE IN ENGLISH." My thought, genius!

Do you ever feel as if your students speak another language? They do indeed! Hence, teachers must learn this language, so to say, and update their instructional repertoire in order to meet their students' needs.

As it relates to academics, every school must utilize a research based and reliable curriculum in all core areas. This curriculum must be aligned directly with the State and College and Career Ready Standards.

It is also critical to employ assessments that are research-based and reliable. Your team must decide what provides you with the information needed to design remediation and enrichment interventions for your students. My team utilizes both norm-referenced along with local benchmarking assessments in the core areas of reading and math to obtain a breadth of academic data from which to make instructional decisions.

Norm-referenced tests provide educators with a global view of how their students perform compared to other students the same age across the country; they are administered at least three times a year. This is valuable information and should be used to set school improvement or Ci3T goals. Local screeners can then be used to monitor student progress on a more regular basis and provide critical information for students needing Tier Two and Three interventions. This data will give you specific information about the effectiveness of current interventions, the quality of curriculum, and the efficacy of instructional strategies that are in place.

Once the data has been aggregated, teams of teachers need ample opportunities to review it and plan for interventions. All decisions should be based on data. Instruction must be specifically designed to target areas of growth or enrichment for students. Data takes the guesswork out of student progress. Teachers will know exactly how their students are performing by monitoring and tracking progress through valid and reliable assessments, which will, in turn, make planning for instruction strategic and targeted.

> *During lunch duty, a third-grade student calls me over to her seat. She inquires as to whether one of our male teacher aides is married. I tell her that he is not. She then asks, "Well, does he have a baby mama?"*
>
> *~ Third Grade!*

We all have choices, including whom we marry, but students have the choice to either engage in instruction or spend their hours at school with their own time fillers that will not enhance their learning or the school's test scores. Educators have instructional choices as well and must employ strategies that actively engage students in the learning process. Of course, the right curriculum must be in place, but instructional strategies and choice are equally important regarding the learning process.

Students must be engaged in order to be learning. The old adage "Practice makes perfect" resonates here, in that learning is not a spectator sport. Students must be actively involved in the learning process in order to be excited about daily lessons, so how do we do this? Here are a few of my go-to's to build teachers' instructional prowess.

EXPLICIT INSTRUCTION BY DR. ANITA ARCHER

There is a common misperception that in order to actively engage students in the learning process, they must be up and moving, working in cooperative groups, building a project, or participating in an experiment that requires resources and time to set up, clean up, and complete. This is not what we are discussing in this chapter, although those are always instructional possibilities. This chapter will highlight easy, effective strategies to implement immediately so that students will have a much higher percentage of responses to instruction throughout the day, thus increasing engagement and achievement and lowering off-task behaviors and interruptions.

Dr. Anita Archer is one of the best speakers and educators I have had the privilege of following over my career. I always seek out her sessions when she speaks at a conference because I know I will leave the session a better-informed educator than when I went into it. Her work is grounded in research and offers educators viable strategies to use in the classroom that will engage both the teacher and the learner, decrease negative behaviors, and increase preferred behaviors, and most of all, these strategies will increase learning and achievement.

Dr. Archer speaks candidly about the importance of creating an environment where students are actively participating in the learning process.[4] All students must be given equitable and frequent opportunities to interact with content, not just the students who raise their hands and volunteer to engage in a lesson. All students must be accountable in the classroom. We have to turn the heat up through participation so that all students know that the expectation in your classroom is one where they will be an active participant.

---

4   Anita Archer and Charles Hughes, *Explicit Instruction: Effective and Efficient Teaching* (New York: Guilford Press, 2011).

It is mid-morning. All students are settled in for the day. I receive a call from a fifth-grade teacher. One of her students has walked out of the building. I head outside and find the student seated across the street on the curb smoking a cigarette. I approach him and let him know that we typically do not allow students to take smoke breaks. He is calm, cool, and collected when he tells me, "I am not on the property, so I am following the rules." Technically he is right. Maybe he will behave better after his "Break."

How do we engage students in the classroom so that they are not tempted to meander outdoors for a smoke, no matter their age? We have to utilize instructional strategies that are intentional and interactive in nature and where the expectation is not simply to finish teaching a lesson but also to provide a classroom culture where learning is the priority.

One analogy Dr. Archer shared during a presentation compared a teacher to a band or orchestra director. If beautiful music is the goal, then the musicians must be directed. The same is true of teachers and students. If learning is the desired outcome, then students must be directed by their teachers.

Dr. Archer has classified the term Active Participation to define strategies teachers can use in their classrooms to replace ineffective strategies such as lectures with more effective and efficient strategies that keep students on the edge of their seats as well as on their toes during instruction.

Active Participation creates a positive learning environment where students are engaged in the learning process. Active Participation occurs when learning is actually visible to the eye. If a principal visits a classroom for observation, and students are quiet and listening to instruction, this does not assure that all of them are actually participating in instruction or learning. In fact, some students may be daydreaming about their next smoke break. Students must be accountable to interact and respond to learning, which will result in improved behavior due to academic participation; they are too busy to be off task and misbehave. As Dr. Archer says, "The magic is in the instruction." Here are some of her magical strategies to increase your fitness level in today's classroom.

WORD OF CAUTION

Although these strategies may sound very easy, and they are, they must be planned, rehearsed, and practiced by both the teacher and the students. Dr. Archer recommends going through teacher manuals and adding ways for students to actively participate in each lesson. Active Participation strategies must be a part of lesson planning. A teacher cannot integrate such strategies with competence if the strategies are not planned and purposeful.

ACTIVE PARTICIPATION STRATEGIES FALL INTO THREE CATEGORIES: ORAL, WRITTEN, AND ACTION

ORAL ACTIVE PARTICIPATION STRATEGIES

- *Choral Responses:* As educators, we all know what choral responses are, but are we utilizing this strategy effectively? If we simply allow a group of students to call out responses, we cannot be assured that all students are actually engaged in learning or if they are just following the lead of others or not involved at all. Here are some strategies to improve the effectiveness of choral responses.

  1. *Signal for Oral Response:* Dr. Archer teaches learners that when she raises her hands in the air with her palms facing outward, this is "Think Time." When she lowers her hands with palms facing upward, this is "Response Time." This strategy replaces having students raise their hands and be called upon individually. All students will be responsible to respond. This strategy is typically used for questions that solicit a short response from students. For example, the teacher may phrase a question to the students, "Who was the first President of the United States?" She will raise her hands and state, "Think Time," and in a brief moment, lower her hands and say, "Response." The

students respond chorally with the response, George Washington. After using this strategy for a few days, teachers will not have to give verbal reminders, simply stating a question and raising your hands will trigger the think and response cues.

2. *I Say, We Say, You Say:* Use this strategy when you are teaching a new strategy or skill.

   I Say: The teacher demonstrates a new strategy or skill. For example, when introducing the sound of a letter in kindergarten, the teacher says or demonstrates the sound to the students.

   We Say: The teacher guides the students as they practice a new skill or strategy. For example, students practice verbalizing a new letter sound together as a group or with partners or a small group. The teacher monitors students as they practice the skill and provides constructive and encouraging feedback.

   You Say: Students practice a skill independently, and the teacher checks for understanding.

3. *Choral Read:* The content for a lesson is on an electronic board visible to all students. Students are directed to read along with the teacher, or the teacher reads some of the verbiage and stops and has the students fill in the last word. Dr. Archer will often say, "Teach with me," when she asks students to read together, which I believe gives them confidence as she promotes them to teacher from student, thus encouraging participation.

4. *Cloze Read:* The teacher reads a sentence and stops at a word, and the students are asked to fill in the blank with the next word in the phrase or sentence. The teacher can give the students a prompt to solicit a choral response from students.

5. *Stand and Deliver:* After students have had time together with a partner to discuss a skill or strategy, they will stand and deliver their response to a prompt. This strategy keeps partners and small groups on task because they know they are accountable to report out to the class.

6. *Examples and Non-Examples:* Students are given time to think and generate examples or non-examples of a skill or strategy presented to them. They then share their ideas with a partner or with the class.

7. *Definitions:* Students are given time to think and then share with a partner, group, or class definitions of vocabulary words, skills, or strategies during a lesson.

8. *Random System for Calling on Students:* Teachers can utilize an old-fashioned system of writing the students' names on tongue blades and pulling the names out of a container to call on students randomly or utilizing an application on a phone that randomly selects students' names, such as Teachers Pick or Pick Me. Students remain engaged due to the fact that they may be called upon to respond.

- *Partners:*

    1. *Assign Numbers:* If a teacher intends to utilize partners as a strategy to provide opportunities for students to respond to instruction, they should number the students, one and two, at the start of the lesson. If there is an uneven number of students, one of the groups will have three people with two number ones or two number twos. The use of partners is particularly effective when students are practicing a skill that has been introduced and demonstrated for them prior to being turned loose with a peer.

    2. *Compare and Contrast and Cause and Effect:* These skills are famous for providing students with guided practice as they are learning a new skill or strategy. Students have to transform information that they have learned into a new format, which encourages higher-level thinking. It can be implied that students would be asked to work with a partner and find similarities and differences about a topic or would be asked to identify how one situation might impact another.

    3. *Sentence Starters:* This strategy will provide students with support as they work together to learn a new concept. Sentence starters should also ask the students to use the information they are learning in their response. For example, if a social studies teacher was teaching about Abraham Lincoln, the students would have a sentence starter that forced them to describe what was being taught, such as "Abraham Lincoln was a transformative President because …"

4. *Explain a Concept:* Just as it sounds, students are asked to explain a concept to a partner, small group, or if they are called on by the teacher such as "Explain to a partner how you would solve this equation."

5. *Count the Number of Ideas Brainstormed with a Partner:* One way to motivate students is to make the learning environment a bit competitive. Teachers can challenge partners to come up with as many ideas as possible about a strategy or skill being taught and then compare numbers between all of the groups.

WRITTEN ACTIVE PARTICIPATION STRATEGIES

- *I Write, We Write, You Write:* This is the same concept as before but is used during lessons that involve any sort of writing. The teacher demonstrates during the "I Write" portion of the lesson. Students practice during the "We Write" portion of the lesson together, and they work independently during the "You Write" portion of the lesson.
- *Dry-Erase Boards or Chromebooks or "Hold Ups":* Students write a response on either a dry-erase board or a Chromebook and are accountable to hold up their response for the teacher to check for understanding.
- *Examples and Non-Examples:* Students are given time to think and generate written examples or non-examples of a skill or strategy presented to them. They then share their ideas with a partner or with the class.
- *Compare and Contrast, Cause and Effect:* Students are asked to work with a partner and find similarities and differences

about a topic or would be asked to identify how one situation might impact another.

- *Enter and Exit Tickets:* Students are asked to provide a written response to a prompt when they enter the classroom or provide a written response to a prompt prior to leaving the class for the day. This information allows the teacher to monitor student progress and check for understanding.

- *Just Two:* Students are asked to respond to a prompt using only two sentences. They then can share with a partner, the class, or the teacher who is using a systemic process to call on students, thus holding them accountable during the lesson.

ACTION PARTICIPATION STRATEGIES

- *I Do, We Do, You Do:* This is the same concept as before but is used during lessons that involve any sort of action or demonstration. The teacher demonstrates during the "I Do" portion of the lesson. Students practice during the "We Do" portion of the lesson, and they work independently during the "You Do" portion of the lesson.

- *Hand on Head:* When it is time to think, ask the students to physically place their hand on their head or forehead. Physically doing this action automatically engages the students in learning.

- *Response Cards:* Students hold up cards with the following possible responses: Yes/No, True/False, A, B, C, D (multiple choice).

- *Dry-Erase Boards or Chromebooks:* Students are accountable to write a response and then either hold up their response so that the teacher can assure they have done the work or share their response with a partner or the class.

- *Stand and Deliver:* When working with partners, the students must stand and deliver their response to a prompt to the class.

- *Hand Signals: Thumbs Up/Down:* Using gestures is a great strategy to use in order to garner a quick read regarding student participation and understanding.

- *Act Out:* Students are asked to act out scenarios or situations with a partner, small group, or the class.

- *Touching and Pointing:* Ask students to touch their screens, follow along with their fingers while reading, and point to correct responses.

- *Facial Expressions:* Ask students to respond to learning with clever facial expressions, thus keeping them actively engaged in the lesson.

- *Find or Draw a Picture Representation:* This strategy forces students to transform learning from one format to another, which is challenging as well as motivating. Giving them the option to draw or search for a picture rules out the concern that some students do not enjoy drawing. I have had my students draw a representation of a story character using their nondominant hand. This is a very challenging activity but puts all students on the same playing field artistically so that students who struggle with art are less intimidated.

- *Electronic Response Systems:* Students can use their computers, clickers, or phones to electronically respond to instruction, thus providing teachers with immediate feedback regarding comprehension.

FORMATIVE ASSESSMENTS

All these strategies naturally embed formative assessments, which allows a teacher to monitor student progress, check for understanding, and determine if material needs to be retaught or if students are ready to proceed to the next skill. The aforementioned strategies provide feedback to teachers and allow them to maintain a pulse on student achievement.

Start Small: It is imperative that a teacher select a few of these strategies to work on at a time. Establishing a routine with these strategies takes time for both the teacher and the students. It also takes time to integrate these strategies into lesson plans. Just as it was important to flag the standards that are to be taught, it is equally important to go through the teacher manuals and note where and when to integrate Active Participation strategies. A concerted effort must be made to plan these activities in order to execute and deliver them with fidelity.

Active Participation strategies are nonnegotiable at my school. No matter the day, time, or classroom I am visiting, I should see students engaged actively in learning. Student participation should be visible to me to the point that I could notate in my observation what the students and teacher are doing. Again, start small. Changing behaviors takes time and effort, but when the results come in, beliefs will be changed as well.

Finally, the utilization of such strategies makes the instructional day so much more fun. Teachers and students are happier because all are busy with teaching and learning rather than watching the clock, dealing with discipline, or, once again, planning your next smoke break.

*What can I do to add to my repertoire to make a
difference in the lives of the children I serve?*

How well you teach equals how well they learn.

—DR. ANITA ARCHER

SUPPORTING BEHAVIOR FOR SCHOOL SUCCESS

The book *Supporting Behavior for School Success*, by Dr. Kathleen Lane, also offers educators a guideline for how to implement seven low-intensity instructional strategies that improve instructional delivery by engaging students in the learning process, which, in turn, improves classroom management. Some of these strategies will not be new to seasoned educators; however, they must be utilized with fidelity to be effective and to make a marked difference in both an increase in academic achievement and a decrease in student disruptions.

LOW-INTENSITY STRATEGIES TO ENSURE STUDENT ENGAGEMENT AND LEARNING AND A DECREASE IN STUDENT MISBEHAVIOR

Strategy	Definition	Implementation
Opportunities to Respond to Instruction: This strategy increases student engagement and decreases misbehavior.	During an instructional period, students must be given purposeful opportunities to react and respond to instruction. These opportunities can be written; oral; choral; a signal such as thumbs up/down; use of response cards such as Agree/Disagree, True or False, or Answer A/B/C/D; responses on whiteboards; interacting with a shoulder partner, the use of Guided Notes; or a Clicker or electronic response system.	Although this sounds easy, the prompts, questions, and the Opportunities to Respond need to be written into lesson plans so that the learning opportunity is not missed. Pre-planning such opportunities will set teachers and students up for success.
Behavior-Specific Praise: This strategy praises students' efforts, grit, and perseverance, thus encouraging them to remain on task and perform academically.	Behavior-Specific Praise is an essential strategy for all students. It is positive feedback to students that references specific and desired behaviors. Praise can be given to individual students or groups of students who are following expectations. This sort of praise creates a positive climate and a healthy relationship between the students and the teacher.	This strategy also sounds simple, but it takes practice. Teachers often praise students for their innate abilities, such as "You are so smart" or "You are very good at math," when they should be reinforcing positive behaviors, such as "You have worked very hard on this project, and it sure shows" or "Thank you for walking in the hallways; you are helping our school to be safe." This sort of praise focuses on the behavior versus innate ability and is much more powerful and effective. We also need to avoid generic praise, such as "Good Job" or "Way to Go," for this sort of praise is far less impactful with students.

Strategy	Definition	Implementation
Active Supervision: This strategy requires the teacher to be up monitoring students while they work. Teachers can question students regarding content in order to assure understanding. Teachers can also remind students of the expectations while they walk about or pre-teach the expectations for independent work at the start of the lesson.	Active Supervision is a preventive strategy that promotes a positive learning environment. Teachers actively monitor students while they work with both verbal and nonverbal cues. Teachers are also engaged in the learning process by walking about the classroom and engaging with students regarding their work and behavior. They have a pulse on the classroom and intervene with corrections as needed.	Teachers' plates are very full, and it is tempting to try to get personal work done when students are working independently. However, in doing so, they take the risk of students becoming off task and misbehaving. Teachers must establish the expectations for each lesson and then actively supervise the students while they work, every lesson, every time.
Instructional Feedback: This strategy asks teachers to be actively engaged while students are working. Teachers redirect or even reteach concepts when needed. The use of positive praise and feedback encourages and motivates students and builds relationships between all parties.	Instructional Feedback should be utilized after Direct Instruction and when students have a basic understanding about the content and are working toward proficiency. Feedback helps both the teachers and the students. Teachers get clarification about student understanding, including misunderstandings, which can then be corrected, and students receive constructive and, oftentimes, positive feedback about their work, thus increasing their intrinsic motivation as well as their ability to persevere on future challenging tasks.	This strategy is very easily implemented but does ask that the teacher is actively involved with students not only during Direct Instruction but when they are working independently as well. Reteaching or corrections may be necessary when students do not understand the expected content. Feedback can correct and guide students in the right direction. Avoid generic feedback such as "Good Job" or "Well Done." In order for students to benefit from this strategy, the feedback must be specific, content oriented and reinforce students' understanding as well as their effort and perseverance.

Strategy	Definition	Implementation
High-Probability Requests: This strategy has a teacher begin a complex lesson with a couple of simple tasks prior to engaging in more difficult or challenging concepts in an effort to build momentum and confidence in learning.	High-Probability Requests is a strategy that has a teacher begin a lesson with two to five EASY tasks in order to build momentum from successful interactions with the curriculum prior to digging into the more challenging material. The interaction with easier tasks increases students' engagement and confidence with the curriculum and makes them more likely to remain engaged when the material becomes more challenging.	These high-probability activities take minimal time to integrate into a lesson plan and have a huge impact. Again, teachers must integrate these strategies into their lesson plans so that the opportunity to engage students is not missed. This is another strategy that may sound easy and could be done on the fly. This is not the case. Purposefully plan these interactions in order to achieve the full benefit of the strategy.
Precorrection: This strategy has the teacher troubleshoot problematic student behavior by pre-teaching the expectations to students.	Precorrection is a strategy that allows teachers to anticipate which lessons may solicit behavioral concerns. In an effort to be proactive rather than reactive, teachers precorrect or remind students of the expectations. Teachers shift from responding to negative behaviors to preventing them altogether through purposeful instruction of the expectations. Teachers anticipate the potential problems before they ever occur and provide students with prompts, support, and reinforcement to prevent the behaviors from happening in the first place.	This strategy takes little time other than to anticipate when and where students might struggle with behavior during a lesson and then front-load the expectations. My staff utilizes the CHAMPS model (Safe and Civil Schools, Randy Sprick, PhD) for this strategy. Before each lesson, they teach the following: C: Conversation: What level of conversation will be allowed during this activity? H: Help: How do students get help during this activity? A: Activity: What tasks should the students be doing? M: Movement: What sort of movement about the classroom is allowed during this activity? P: Participation: What behaviors should students display to be participating correctly? S: This stands for SUCCESS. If we follow the aforementioned expectations, we will all be CHAMPS!

Strategy	Definition	Implementation
Instructional Choice: This strategy has the teacher provide the students with a couple or a few options regarding how to complete an assignment, thus giving the students some control regarding their work.	There are two ways to offer instructional choices to students. The first is the easiest. Provide students with more than one way to complete an assignment, such as working at their desk or in the reading corner, using markers or colored pencils, working with a peer or by oneself, or sitting in a chair or on a beanbag. The second way to integrate Instructional Choice takes a bit more planning. A teacher provides students with a variety of manners in which to complete a project such as a written report versus a YouTube video, writing a song, or creating an artistic version of the content. Instructional Choice allows students to have some control over their learning and reduces negative behaviors.	Instructional choices make learning fun. It is easy to provide choices, such as pen colors or seating options, but it takes planning to offer students a variety of manners in which to complete an assignment, but it is worth it because the students will buy into the work they have to do. HyperDocs are a great way to provide students with instructional choices. They are similar to a Tic-Tac-Toe board but are electronic and provide students with academic choices in each box. Links can be added to the boxes allowing the students to view videos or create electronic projects. If this option feels daunting, offer students two options of how to respond to the curriculum. Start there, and let this strategy evolve as it becomes more comfortable and the norm.

Each year for the spring concert, the kindergarten class comes dressed as what they want to be when they grow up. A mother and her son arrive for the event, and he is dressed as a lion. I look at her, and she says, "I do not have the heart to tell him that this isn't possible." The show goes on!

No matter what children want to be when they grow up, it is the job of educators to best prepare them for that role even if the role is a far cry from reality. In order to accomplish this lofty goal, students must not only be highly engaged in the learning process through Active Participation strategies, but they must also be challenged to think and problem solve at high levels so that they can compete in a competitive and challenging work market.

When students are challenged and engaged in the learning process, there will be an increase in academic achievement and a decrease in student discipline. Each spring, when students take part in state assessments, they are asked to respond to questions that are rigorous in nature. We must align instruction not only to the assessment expectations if we hope for our students to perform well on this battery of tests but also in preparing them to be successful in the workforce.

My school district implements Webb's Depth of Knowledge as a guide for how to plan lessons that challenge students to think and problem solve at rigorous levels. No matter the academic level or struggles of a student, they all must encounter learning strategies that stretch their thinking capacity. I tell my staff, the content can be made easier, but all students must be exposed to strategies that cause them to think analytically. Let's take a look at Webb's Depth of Knowledge.

WEBB'S DEPTH OF KNOWLEDGE

Webb's Depth of Knowledge was founded by Norman Webb at the Wisconsin Center for Education Research. His research was closely linked to his predecessor, Benjamin Bloom. Both these scholars studied cognition, or the ways people learn and acquire new information.

Bloom's Taxonomy has been around for decades. We first must understand this framework prior to integrating Webb's Depth of Knowledge into our instructional arsenal. Bloom and his team of researchers at the University of Chicago created a cognitive framework for teaching and learning. There were three domains for this framework: Cognitive, Affective, and Psychomotor. For the purpose of this book, we are only going to examine the Cognitive Domain. Whew!

When first introduced, Bloom reported that there were six classification levels in his cognitive learning model. They were the following: *Knowledge, Comprehension, Application, Analysis, Synthesis, and Evaluation.* The first three levels were considered lower-level thinking applications, whereas the final three levels required students to delve deeper and utilize more rigorous thinking strategies to think and problem solve.

Bloom's work was revised in 2001, when researchers, including some from the original team, tried to make the Taxonomy more user-friendly to educators by labeling the levels with verbs rather than nouns so that teachers could easily see how to integrate these levels of learning into their lesson plans with ease. The domains were renamed to verbs and were changed to the following: *Remember, Understand, Apply, Analyze, Evaluate, and Create.* Again, the first three domains require lower-level thinking strategies, whereas the final three levels require higher levels of problem-solving.

Bloom's Taxonomy

CREATING	**EVALUATING**	**ANALYZING**
USE INFO TO CREATE SOMETHING NEW	CRITICALLY EXAMINE INFO & MAKE JUDGEMENTS	TAKE INFO APART & EXPLORE RELATIONSHIPS
design, build, plan, construct, produce, devise, invent	judge, critique, test, defend, criticize	categorize, examine, organize, compare/contrast

APPLYING
USE INFO IN A NEW (BUT SIMILAR) FORM
use, diagram, make a chart, draw, apply, solve, calculate

UNDERSTANDING
UNDERSTANDING & MAKING SENSE OUT OF INFO
interpret, summarize, explain, infer, paraphrase, discuss

REMEMBERING
FIND OR REMEMBER INFO
list, find, name, identify, locate, describe, memorize, define

Norman Webb has taken Bloom's Taxonomy and reconfigured it. He defines Depth of Knowledge as "the degree or complexity of knowledge that the content curriculum standards and expectations require." In other words, lesson plans teachers construct must ensure that the assignments are cognitively demanding enough to match the standards so that students learn how to thrive and succeed in the academic arena and will be prepared to interact in a complex world and workforce.

Webb's Depth of Knowledge highlights four levels of learning:

1. RECALL: Students are asked to take part in basic recall of information, such as facts, definitions, terms, or procedures. They will list; tell; answer the questions that involve Who, What, When, Where, and Why; recall; recite; or report.

2. SKILLS AND CONCEPTS: Students follow multiple steps to come to a conclusion. They infer, categorize, predict, modify, classify, and identify cause and effect as a few examples.

3. STRATEGIC THINKING: Students are challenged with more rigor at this level. They might be asked to revise, critique, hypothesize, cite evidence, compare, construct, differentiate, and investigate.

4. EXTENDED THINKING: This level provides students with the greatest amount of rigor. They might be asked to design, connect, synthesize, apply concepts, analyze, create, and prove. Educators need to concentrate on creating lessons that fall into Webb's Depth of Knowledge, or DOK as we call them, three and four. Again the content can be adjusted, but all students must learn how to work through rigorous challenges. There are multiple free visuals on the web that list verbs to consider when lesson planning. Each year, I look for a new visual, copy and laminate it, and distribute it to teachers to keep at their desks to use when creating lesson plans.

Webb's Depth of Knowledge Wheel

You might ask, am I saying that all lessons must be at Webb's Depth of Knowledge levels three and four? Not at all! When introducing new information, skills, and strategies, teachers may need to utilize activities from levels one and two. However, each day, students should have to grapple with intellectual challenges, so there needs to be a healthy balance of activities and rigor provided to them.

CLASSROOM INSTRUCTION THAT WORKS, ROBERT MARZANO, DEBRA PICKERING, AND JANE POLLOCK[5]

The authors, Robert Marzano (or Bob, as I refer to him with my staff, because surely we are on a first name basis after all the years I have been reading his work and applying his strategies in my schools and classrooms), Debra Pickering, and Jane Pollock, created a list of nine instructional strategies that really do work. They identified the strategies through meta-analyses that allowed them to combine research results from multiple studies to determine the effectiveness the strategies have on student achievement.

In order to see gains in student achievement, we must utilize research-based instructional strategies. The ten most effective strategies, as it relates to student achievement according to Bob and colleagues, are as follows and are summarized from my understanding and interpretation of the authors' work.

IDENTIFYING SIMILARITIES AND DIFFERENCES

Comparing and contrasting subject matter is an effective strategy that builds students' academic capacity. Having students compare, classify, and work with metaphors and analogies forces them to interact with information in a vigorous manner. The use of graphic organizers, such as Venn Diagrams, a Comparison Matrix, Time-Sequence Pattern Organizers, or Classification Organizers, is highly effective when teaching these skills.

---

5   Ceri B. Dean and Robert J. Marzano, *Classroom Instruction That Works: Research-Based Strategies for Increasing Student Achievement* (Boston, Mass: Pearson Education, 2001).

METAPHORS

Definition: A comparison of two things that are unrelated

The math test was a beast! The school lunch was garbage! Our teacher is a magician!

Write a metaphor in each text box advertising something you like, such as a brand of shoes, OR

Write a metaphor in each text box describing something you are good at, such as a sport.

WORD ANALOGIES

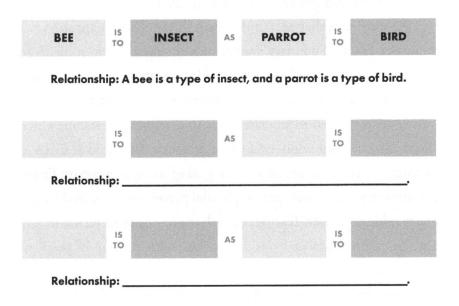

Relationship: A bee is a type of insect, and a parrot is a type of bird.

Relationship: _____.

Relationship: _____.

There are a plethora of graphic organizers for all these skills and strategies free on the web. Have fun exploring, and then challenge your students regularly with these critical skills.

SUMMARIZING AND NOTE-TAKING

SUMMARIZING

Summarizing information is a powerful strategy that forces students to not only interact with information but also prioritize its meaning in their own words. When summarizing, an exercise teachers can use with students is to have them read a passage and delete information by drawing lines through sentences that are not critical to the meaning of the work. Students can also write in words or sentences that make the information clearer to them. Finally, students determine what information to keep from the passage in an effort to identify the key ideas that give the passage meaning. This is a great exercise because it forces students to analyze a passage of writing critically and challenges them to think and problem solve at high levels.

Another tool that aids in the instruction of summarization is a Summary Frame. Summary Frames provide questions to students to help them organize and identify meaning in writing, videos, or any instructional activity that requires summarization. Questions for the frames are presented to students prior to the start of a lesson, which allows them to contemplate the questions while they read or listen to instruction. The final product or the goal of using a Summary Frame is a summary, a sentence, paragraph, oral presentation, or in the form of a graphic organizer. Teachers can ask students to complete this task together, with guidance from the teacher, with a group of peers, or independently.

There are six categories of Summary Frames as follows:

- *The Narrative Frame*
  This frame is used for works of fiction. Questions focus on the characters from a story, the setting, the initiating event, responses to the event, the goal set by the main characters, how the characters accomplish the goal, and the resolution to the story.

NARRATIVE SUMMARY FRAME

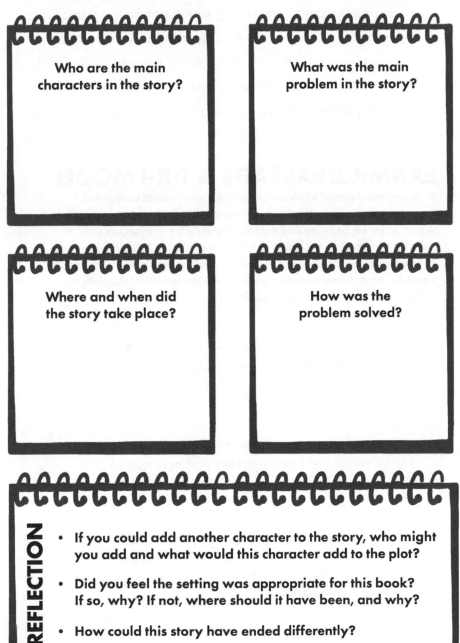

Who are the main
characters in the story?

What was the main
problem in the story?

Where and when did
the story take place?

How was the
problem solved?

REFLECTION

- If you could add another character to the story, who might you add and what would this character add to the plot?

- Did you feel the setting was appropriate for this book? If so, why? If not, where should it have been, and why?

- How could this story have ended differently?

- *The Topic-Restriction-Illustration Frame, or the TRI Frame*

  The Topic-Restriction-Illustration Frame is used when examining expository writing. Questions for this frame focus on the T (topic) of the writing and the R (Restriction) or what information from the writing narrows or limits the writing, and the I (Illustration) asks students to identify examples from the text that illustrate either the topic or the restriction from the writing.

EXAMPLE PASSAGE & T-R-I MODEL

Have you ever heard of a bearcat? Is it a bear, or is it a cat? Well, it actually is a small to medium-sized mammal that got its name because it has the body of a bear and the face of a cat. A bearcat can be found in the jungles of southeast Asia, but they are difficult to spot due to the fact that they are nocturnal and spend much of their time high up in the trees. Hence, it has been a challenge to learn much about them. Bearcats may also be hard to find because they are decreasing in population due to being hunted for their meat and medicinal purposes. Also, they are declining as a species because their habitats have been disturbed thus reducing their food source. Bearcats are a fascinating animal of which little is known.

T
Bearcats are endangered mammals that look like a cross between a bear and a cat.

R
It is difficult to learn about the bearcat due to its habits and the fact that they are endangered.

I
Bearcats are nocturnal and live high up in trees; hence they're difficult to observe. The bearcat is endangered because of being hunted for meat and medicinal purposes. Their habitat has been disrupted.

Summary: A bearcat is a mammal that looks like a cross between a bear and a cat. They are difficult to learn about because of their habits and that they are endangered animals.

TOPIC-RESTRICTION-ILLUSTRATION

T: What is the topic of the passage?

R: What information from the passage restricts the topic from the passage?

I: What information from the passage illustrates either the topic or the restriction of the topic?

- *The Definition Frame*

    The Definition Frame asks students to define or describe a word or concept they are studying. Questions for this frame ask students to classify words into categories or groups. They compare and contrast vocabulary or concepts to other words or ideas in the same category. For example, a daisy and a rose are both flowers and fall into the same category. How are they similar, and how are they different?

DEFINITION FRAME

Draw a Picture of the Word or Concept

Category of Word or Concept

Non-Examples of the Word or Concept

ITEM TO BE DEFINED

Words or Concepts in the Same Category

List a New Way to Use it, or a Personal Experience with it.

Differences from Others in the Same Category

CATEGORIZE AND CLASSIFY

Categorize the words below into groups, and then classify the name of the group.

teacher desk recess principal pencil music custodian crayon math secretary notebook science student computer reading

Category: _____

Category: _____

Category: _____

- *The Argumentation Frame*

  The Argumentation Frame asks students to read text and identify information that leads to some sort of claim.

Students identify the claim as well as what evidence from the text supports or limits the claim.

THE AUGMENTATION FRAME

What evidence is presented that leads to a potential claim?

What is the focus of the claim being made?

What evidence is presented to support the claim?

What restrictions are made about the claim?

- *The Problem/Solution Frame*

  The Problem/Solution Frame asks students to identify problems and potential solutions in text or content. Taking it one step further, this frame also asks students to select which solution they believe from the content has the greatest potential to be successful.

PROBLEM-SOLUTION FRAME

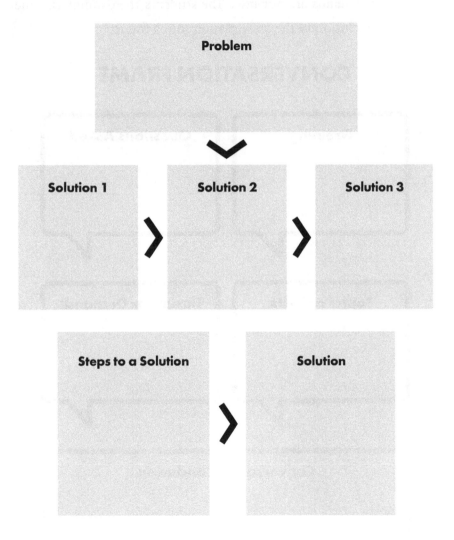

- *Conversation Frame*

Conversation Frames are used when stories are told in the form of a conversation. Students are asked to identify how the characters greeted one another; the content of the conversation and how the conversation progressed, including facts discussed by the characters, requests, demands, or threats made by the characters; and what consequences will occur if demands are not met. The students then summarize the conclusion of the conversation into a frame.

CONVERSATION FRAME

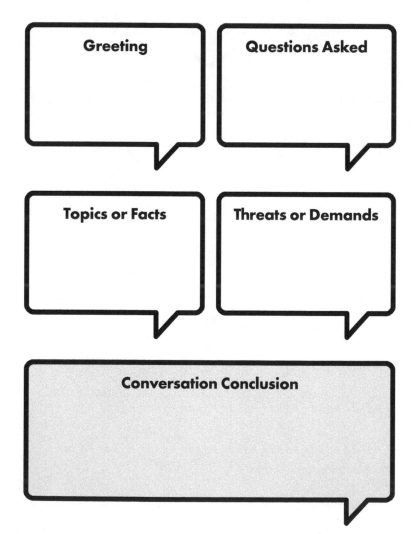

NOTE-TAKING

Note-taking requires students to summarize; hence, summarizing and note-taking piggyback on one another. There are a variety of effective ways to teach note-taking. Students should learn how to take notes in a variety of formats. There are several formats that are extremely effective.

- *Teacher Template:* The teacher provides students with notes in an outlined form, thus teaching them what note-taking looks like and providing them with the content that needs to be learned.
- *Informal Outline:* Students list the main ideas and use indentations for ideas and details that fall under each category.
- *Webbing:* Students put the main ideas into the larger circles and the ideas and details related to the main idea in smaller circles. Students connect the related circles with lines. This type of note-taking provides students with more of a visual representation of their thoughts and ideas.
- *Combination Notes:* Students divide their notes into three sections by drawing a line down the center of their page, leaving enough room to draw another line across the bottom of the page. On the left side of the page, they would use the Informal Outline format and record their main ideas and details with indentions. On the right side of their paper, they use visual representations of their notes such as the Web circles and lines. The bottom of their page is reserved for summary statements.

Both summarizing and note-taking are critical skills for students to acquire to be successful academically. It is essential that teachers integrate them into their arsenal of instructional strategies.

REINFORCING EFFORT AND PROVIDING RECOGNITION

I am beyond thrilled that this strategy made the top nine strategies regarding student achievement because I have always asserted that a positive and proactive approach with students not only helps their behavior but also improves their achievement. Thanks to Bob, I have the research to back up this assertion.

REINFORCING EFFORT

Effort, not innate ability, is where the money is as it relates to teacher reinforcement with students. The importance of effort is also noted in the work of Carol Dweck (Mindset) with her studies about the concept of Growth Mindset. Teachers must reinforce the importance of effort to their students. Students should also assess themselves regarding the amount of effort they exert in class as well. Reinforcement statements such as "You're so good at math" versus "Your effort on that math project was amazing, no wonder it turned out so well" demonstrate the difference in the delivery style of reinforcement. The first example teaches children that they are born with innate skills that are fixed rather than the idea that effort can have a positive impact on growth because the brain is a muscle, and with practice, anything can be learned, as highlighted in the second statement. We must teach our students that anything is possible and that their effort is key to their success.

PROVIDING RECOGNITION

Recognition of students can come in many forms and is highly effective as an instructional strategy.

- *Personalizing Recognition:* Students set personal goals and are assessed on their own growth rather than being compared to the performance of others, such as an honor roll. I do not believe in maintaining an honor roll. It is often the same students on the honor roll semester after semester, which crushes the spirit of those not attaining such a lofty goal. Rather, recognize students who attain personal goals each semester, and then sit back and see how the climate and culture change to one where all students feel as if they have potential in the classroom.

- *Pause, Prompt, and Praise:* When working with a student who is struggling with a concept, ask the student to pause and identify why they are struggling. The teacher then provides a prompt or suggestion to the student to assist in moving forward. When the student continues to work and demonstrates competence, the teacher swoops in with praise, and I would recommend using praise revolving around the student's effort.

- *Concrete Symbols of Recognition:* The teacher utilizes items such as stickers, tickets, electronic points, coupons, or treats as a few examples of concrete recognition. I recommend including verbal praise regarding students' effort when delivering concrete recognition. Twice as powerful!

HOMEWORK AND PRACTICE

GUIDELINES FOR HOMEWORK

- Homework has been found to have a positive impact on students at all grade levels. The rule of thumb regarding the amount of homework nightly is determined by the age of the child. Children should be able to do homework for a period of time that is ten times their assigned grade level. For example, if a child is in second grade, they could be expected to work on homework for twenty minutes.

- Parents should facilitate a time and place for homework completion and provide minimal assistance with the content of the homework.
- Purpose of Homework: Teachers must communicate, and students must understand the purpose for the homework assignment. Are they to practice a skill, finish an assignment from class, or do an assignment that is an extension of work done at school?
- Homework should be graded, or feedback to students regarding their work should be provided.

GUIDELINES FOR HOMEWORK PRACTICE

- In order to learn any new skill, opportunities for practice must be offered.
- Practice should include opportunities to build skill, accuracy, and speed.
- Focused Practice: This form of practice has students focus on one idea or concept of a multistep problem in order to fine-tune skills in that area.
- Students must have a competent understanding of a skill prior to practice at home; otherwise, they may practice the skill incorrectly.

NONLINGUISTIC REPRESENTATIONS

Students are often asked to interact with information linguistically, but experiencing content in a nonlinguistic manner provides students with an alternative way to experience learning and has a positive impact on achievement.

The following are research-based strategies regarding Nonlinguistic Representations:

- Graphic Organizers ask students to organize information into a visual representation or pattern. There are six patterns that are most effective.

    1. Descriptive Patterns: Descriptive patterns ask students to organize facts about people, places, things, and events. Next is a typical example of this sort of graphic organizer.

DESCRIPTIVE PATTERN ORGANIZER

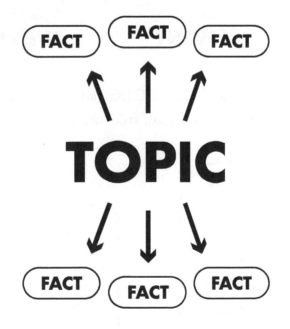

**Organize facts about people, places, or events
without concern for time or sequence.**

2. Time-Sequence Patterns: Time-Sequence Patterns ask students to place events in logical order.

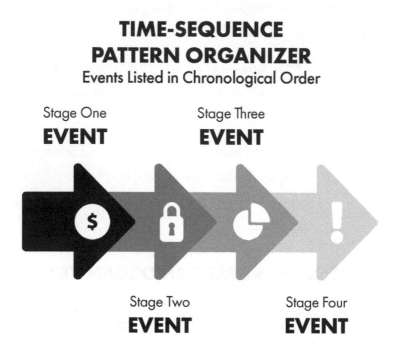

TIME-SEQUENCE PATTERN ORGANIZER
Events Listed in Chronological Order

Stage One
EVENT

Stage Three
EVENT

Stage Two
EVENT

Stage Four
EVENT

3. Process/Cause and Effect Patterns: Process/Cause and Effect Patterns ask students to identify factors that contribute to a specific outcome.

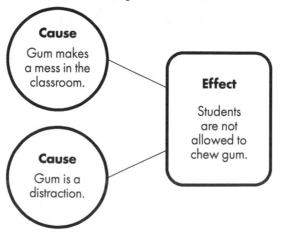

Cause
Gum makes a mess in the classroom.

Effect
Students are not allowed to chew gum.

Cause
Gum is a distraction.

4. Episode Patterns: Episode Patterns ask students to organize information about events such as the setting, duration, people, events, and the cause and effect of the events.

EPISODE GRAPHIC ORGANIZER

Organizes information or an episode into categories: Setting, Time Period, Place, Duration, Time Sequence, Cause and Effect, and People.

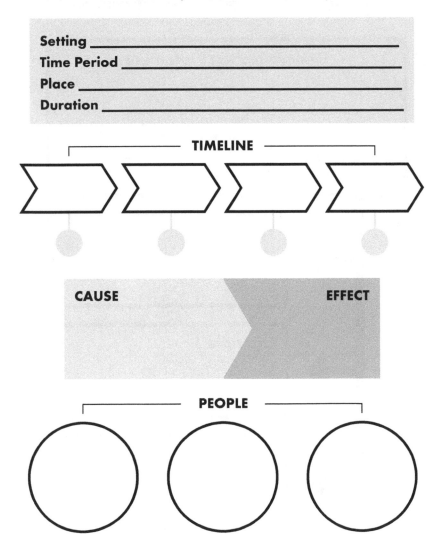

Setting _____
Time Period _____
Place _____
Duration _____

TIMELINE

CAUSE   EFFECT

PEOPLE

5. Generalization/Principle Patterns: Generalization/Principle Patterns ask students to organize information beginning with a general statement followed by examples that support the statement.

GENERALIZATION/PRINCIPLE PATTERN ORGANIZER

Organizes Information into a General Statement with Supporting Examples

Generalization Statement

Example

Example

Example

6. Concept Patterns: Concept Patterns ask students to organize information based off of a word or phrase that represents categories of people, places, things, and events.

CONCEPT PATTERNS

Organizes information around a concept that represents classes or categories of people, places, things, and events.

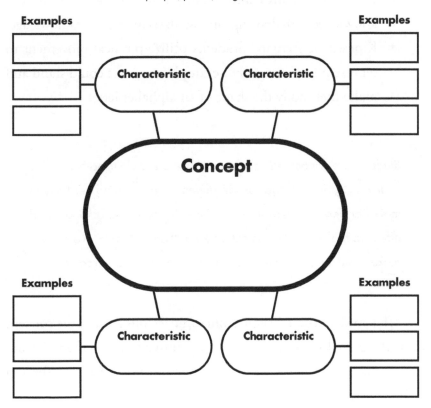

- Physical Models: Students create a physical representation of what they are learning.
- Mental Pictures: Ask students to close their eyes and imagine themselves in a new situation. Ask them to think about what they might see, smell, hear, or taste and then envision themselves in the situation you have drummed up in their imaginations.
- Drawing Pictures and Pictographs: Students represent knowledge with drawings and symbols to represent knowledge.
- Kinesthetic Activity: Students utilize physical movement to represent knowledge. For example, students could stand and make their body the shape of an alphabet letter.

Students are concerned because a classmate is claiming her desk is haunted. Upon investigation, the student is found using her belly to make her desk "move on its own." Cleverly, she is also adding sound effects to make the situation extremely authentic. Maybe we need to make room for one more "invisible" student in our classroom?

This student could benefit from some lessons around the concept of working well with others, and cooperative learning is an instructional strategy that provides such opportunities and makes the top of Bob's list.

COOPERATIVE LEARNING

JOHNSON AND JOHNSON

Cooperative learning is a way of grouping students for instructional purposes. This is a highly effective strategy because the students tend to be actively engaged in the learning process. There are several guidelines for how to best utilize this strategy:

- Mix up the ways in which you group students and avoid grouping by ability.
- Cooperative Learning can be used informally (turn to a neighbor and share an idea), formally (students are placed into a group to complete a project), and through base grouping (students are grouped for a semester or a year for classes such as homeroom or seminar where students do informal activities to get to know one another).[6]
- Cooperative Learning is more effective when groups are kept to small numbers and not overused.

SETTING OBJECTIVES AND PROVIDING FEEDBACK

It is critical that teachers let students know not only what it is that they are expected to learn but also to set goals to attain such learning. Some ways of implementing these strategies are as follows.

- Have students set goals for each unit of study.
- Create contracts for students that identify what goals the students have to achieve throughout a unit.
- Provide feedback that is corrective in nature. Students need to know what they are doing well and where they need to improve.
- Feedback should be delivered in a timely fashion.
- Feedback should be specific to what the students were expected to learn. A percentage score on a test does not provide specific

---

6   David W. Johnson et al., *Cooperative Learning in the Classroom* (Alexandria, VA: Association for Supervision and Curriculum Development, 1994).

feedback and is not as effective as feedback that specifies changes to be made or what students did well.

- Students can take part in tracking and monitoring their own progress. Feedback does not have to come solely from the teacher.

GENERATING AND TESTING HYPOTHESES

There are five types of recommended activities for students to employ in order to build their skill level in the area of generating and testing hypotheses:

- *Systems Analysis:* Have students assess what would happen if one aspect of a system (ecosystems, governmental systems, or any other type of system) were changed. Have students generate hypotheses about such changes.
- *Problem-Solving:* For this process, students are asked to identify a problem to solve, explain the barriers to solving the problem, pose solutions, try solutions, and then reflect on whether their hypothesis was correct or not.
- *Historical Investigation:* Students analyze historical events and pose theories as to what potentially led up to an event that had historical relevance. They need to describe the event, identify the facts and/or disagreements known about the event, and then pose a hypothesis about what they believe contributed to the event or even actions that could have been done to change the outcome historically.
- *Invention:* Students must hypothesize an idea for an invention, investigate how it might work, design a plan, and then test the hypothesis to see if the idea indeed worked.

- *Experimental Inquiry:* Students observe something that is of interest to them. They brainstorm theories regarding their observation and explain what they observed. They then make a hypothesis of how they could apply what they observed to a similar situation. They set up experiments and test the hypothesis and explain the results.

As I am conducting my morning walk-through observations, a fifth-grade teacher calls me into her room. She says she did not know that she was assigned a new student. I tell her that to my knowledge, she does not have a new student. She points to a little girl seated at a desk. This is not a new fifth-grade student but a current second-grade student. I walk over to her and ask why she is in the wrong classroom. She says, "I am not in the wrong classroom. I want to be in band class, and fifth-grade kids get to go to band. This is my new class." This is not music to my ears.

This student may have missed her cue, but you do not have to miss yours! The next strategy on Bob's list has to do with activating students' prior knowledge through the use of Cues, Questions, and Advance Organizers.

CUES, QUESTIONS, AND ADVANCE ORGANIZERS

Educators use Cues, Questions, and Advance Organizers when teaching with the purpose of activating students' prior knowledge so that students think about their understanding of content before expanding their knowledge with new content. Teachers begin a lesson by providing students with information they already know about a topic and tie it to the new information that is to be taught. This is done in an effort to activate students' prior knowledge.

- *Cues:* Cues ask students to think about content with their current knowledge before experiencing the new content. Cues can be as simple as verbal descriptions of what students already know prior to a new lesson or more extensive such as completing a KWL chart where a teacher has students identify what they already know about a subject (K) and what they want to learn about a subject (W), and once the lesson or unit is complete, students return to the chart and record what they learned (L).

- *Questions That Elicit Inferences:* Teachers pose questions about new content that asks students to think about things, people, actions, events, and states of being related to the content in order to activate prior knowledge.

- *Analytic Questions:* Teachers pose questions that ask students to critique or analyze information in an effort to activate prior knowledge. There are three formats to consider with this type of questioning: (1) Analyzing Errors: Students respond to questions that have them assess if content has errors, is misleading, or could be improved; (2) Constructing Support: Students respond to questions that have them support the content with examples or assert the limitations of the content being taught with examples; and (3) Analyzing Perspectives: Students respond to questions that assess if the content is good, bad, or neutral or describe the reasoning backing the new content, all in an effort to activate prior knowledge.

• *Advance Organizers:* Teachers use information that students already know to help them to learn new information. Teachers can tell stories to set the stage for new learning (Narrative Advance Organizer), describe the new content that is to be taught (Expository Advance Organizer), or ask students to skim information before delving into the work of new learning.

Interesting, did you notice that many of these strategies fall into levels three and four of Webb's Depth of Knowledge? I sure did! These are the strategies needed in today's classrooms to keep students actively engaged in the learning process so that they are not off task and misbehaving.

The office receives an emergency call through the campus radio. A substitute physical education teacher is calling for help on the baseball diamond due to a serious injury. The school nurse and I race out to be of assistance only to find a familiar face on the ground with a smirk at the ready. The PE teacher explains that he asked the class to run to the fence, touch it, and return to the starting point. This young man has a prosthetic leg and makes a habit to turn it around backward whenever a substitute is in the house. Expect the unexpected!

For any lesson, setting the stage for success is necessary, such as letting substitute teachers know about students' repetitive antics! Instructional decisions play an integral role in the success of teaching, and the text, *CHAMPS*, offers viable ideas to educators to assure such success and prevent the unexpected from ever occurring.

CHAMPS: A PROACTIVE AND POSITIVE APPROACH TO CLASSROOM MANAGEMENT[7]

JESSICA SPRICK, DR. RANDY SPRICK, JACOB EDWARDS, AND CRISTY COUGHLIN

Dr. Randy Sprick, Safe and Civil Schools, is not only an exceptional writer, but a comedic speaker who is filled with a wealth of knowledge and experience of how to best work with students and teachers as it relates to classroom management; however, a portion of his text is dedicated to instructional decisions since how teachers teach is directly related to how students behave. The book *CHAMPS* is a staple on my shelf as well as a go-to for a staff book study and professional development.

EFFECTIVE INSTRUCTIONAL DECISIONS

A daily schedule that is posted and visible to all students is a great way to kick off each school day with success in mind. Post pandemic, students need reassurance as to what their day is going to look like. Posting the schedule and referring to it during transitions help prepare

---

7   Randy S. Sprick and Keba Baldwin, *CHAMPS: A Proactive & Positive Approach to Classroom Management* (Eugene, OR: Pacific Northwest Publishing, 2009).

students for what to expect during the day, which alleviates stress for those feeling anxious.

Once the daily schedule has been prepared, teachers then design lessons for the content they are responsible to teach. The strategies selected have a direct impact on student behavior, and the following areas should be considered:

- The daily schedule must provide students with a variety of activities. Too much Direct Instruction will result in bored and off-task students. Assuring that the students have opportunities to interact with the curriculum throughout each day in diverse opportunities is a recipe for success. Lessons should be balanced with teacher-directed learning, cooperative learning, independent or guided practice, discussions, partner work, the use of manipulatives, technology, and verbal and physical responses from students as a few examples.

- Consider the maturity level of the students you serve. For example, some groups of students can handle cooperative activities better than others, so the teacher must be mindful of how to best engage all levels of students.

- The teacher must also consider their own skill set as it relates to instruction. What are your strengths, and where could you develop stronger skills keeping in mind that the days where teachers lecture to students all day are behind us? We must adapt to the times and find active ways for students to engage in the learning process.

- Teachers tend to lean heavily on strategies that they are comfortable using; however, too much of anything is not good. For example, the overuse of teacher lectures will certainly result in poor behavior from the students.

In an effort for the teacher to enjoy teaching and the student to enjoy learning, utilize a variety of instructional strategies that actively engage students in the learning process. Post the schedule daily, teach the expectations for each activity, and supervise vigilantly while monitoring student progress and providing specific feedback for their success.

STRATEGIES TO CONSIDER WHEN LESSON PLANNING

- Direct Instruction
- Cooperative Learning
- Partners of Peer Work
- Guided Practice
- Independent Practice
- Graphic Organizers
- Student Movement
- Webb's Depth of Knowledge, Level Three and Four Activities
- Vocabulary
- Summarizing
- Compare and Contrast
- Learning Centers
- Cues and Questions to Activate Prior Knowledge
- Close Read
- Manipulatives
- Identifying Similarities and Differences
- Guest Speaker
- Generating and Testing a Hypothesis
- Note-Taking
- Debate

- Formative and Summative Assessments
- Flexible Grouping
- Role Playing
- Goal Setting
- Journaling
- Concept Mapping
- Higher-Level Questioning
- Academic Games
- Breakout Boxes
- Case Studies
- Choral Responses
- Charades
- CRISS Strategies
- Art Expression
- Technology
- Flipgrid
- Entry and Exit Tickets
- Jigsaw
- KWL
- Inquiry-Based Learning
- Phonics
- STEM
- Sentence Starters
- Think-Pair-Share
- Author's Chair
- Writer's Workshop
- Zoom
- Homework Practice
- Visualization
- Field Trips

- Experiential Learning
- Simulation
- Brainstorming
- Talking Circles
- Blended Learning

No matter the instructional strategy, the teacher must set the tone and define and teach the expectations for the lesson. Dr. Sprick and team recommend teaching and utilizing the acronym CHAMPS prior to the start of every lesson.

C: Conversation: Defines the level of conversation that is allowed during the lesson.

H: Help: How do students solicit help during the lesson?

A: Activity: The task or objective for the lesson.

M: Movement: What sort of movement is allowed during the lesson?

P: Participation: What will it look like if a student is participating appropriately?

S: Success: If we follow the CHAMPS guidelines, we will experience SUCCESS!

It takes only a few moments at the start of every lesson to teach and review the expectations. Some teachers have the CHAMPS acronym on an electronic slide and fill in the expectations as they review them with the students. Others use sentence charts and cards or a dry-erase board to display the expectations. Practicing or modeling the expectations is another way to reinforce the expectations. Teaching and displaying the expectations for every lesson greatly enhance the quality of instruction and learning. Let's all be CHAMPS!

HOMEWORK AND GRADING PRACTICES

One of the biggest areas of concern for teachers revolves around the completion of homework. To begin with, homework should be an extension of the work done in the classroom, and the students should be capable of practicing the skill on their own. If they are not somewhat competent in the skill, working on it at home incorrectly will only cause both teacher and student more heartache.

Teachers should consider the socioeconomic status of their class when determining the amount of emphasis that is placed on homework. Some students may have no support from home as well as no access to the internet or a computer. Some students may have to care for younger siblings after school and into the evening, and others may have to work jobs.

So many teachers spend their day chasing late assignments and become so frustrated when students' grades are low due to their lack of attention to homework. Perhaps, placing less value on having homework assignments and more of an emphasis on whether or not the students comprehend the content is the answer? Determine how much of a grade should rest on homework completion. If homework is the most common form of grade in your gradebook, you may want to reconsider the weight you are placing on something that takes place outside of your control. The purpose of a homework assignment is to monitor students' progress, not to assess their understanding.

Homework completion is a life skill and one that will help students who choose to go on to a postsecondary education program. Start with small assignments, and teach students your routines and expectations about homework and late work. Have students set goals and celebrate successes when they submit their work on time. Decide your expectations for late work and what the consequences will be when work is not done in a timely fashion or at all, but be mindful of the obstacles some students face as it relates to being able to complete work outside of school and the impact it has when they are failing your class due to homework completion. Quit chasing your tail, and make the system manageable for you and your students.

GRADING PRACTICES

My favorite type of grading system comes from my reading about Growth Mindset and the work of Carol Dweck. If a student is not receiving an "A" or "B" in a subject, they receive the grade "Not Yet." Our education system may not be ready for such a quantum leap, but the fact that this sort of grading system does not communicate to any child that they are a failure certainly sets them up for success.

The CHAMPS approach to grading practices has us question the practice of assigning zeros due to the level of impact just one zero has on a child's grade. Even if a child fails, they receive 50 percent credit. Some teachers have adopted the 50 percent zero. This is controversial because a student earning a zero most likely did not do 50 percent of the work; however, it is something to consider to protect the self-esteem of students who earn failing grades. Grades provide teachers with information about how students are understanding content, and educators should use this information to drive interventions and instruction. Curves are unfair and should not be used.

Finally, it would greatly benefit students' self-esteem if effort were to be an integral part of any grade. When students put a great deal of effort into an assignment, that effort should be recognized and honored. It also sends a clear message to students that their grades rest not only on their academic capacity to perform and that if they work hard, that effort will be noted.

ACADEMIC SCREENERS FOR DATA INTERPRETATION

NORM-REFERENCED SCREENERS

- Aimsweb
- Fastbridge
- MAP
- State Assessments
- ACT, PSAT, SAT
- Accuplacer (Technical School, Community College Entrance Tests)
- ASVAB (Military Enlistment)

LOCAL SCREENERS

- Fountas and Pinnell Reading Benchmarking
- STAR Reading
- Assessments Included in Curriculum: Ancillary Materials
- Special Education Evaluation Referrals and Assessments
- District or State Writing Assessments

It is the start of a school day. I receive a frantic call from the grandfather of one of my kindergarten students. He is refusing to come to school and is sitting on top of his grandmother to prevent her from

> *being able to bring him, again. This is an unusually large kinder-garten student. I relay to the family that once I get the other students settled in for the day, I will send our school security officer over to pick him up for school. They are relieved. I head out to the buses to greet students, and who do I see drive by me with a huge grin and a wave? The kindergarten student. Yes, he is driving the car! My jaw drops open in astonishment. I alert our officer that the situation may be a bit more urgent than expected.*

Of course, academics are critical to the success of any child, but the other domains are equally as critical and, in my opinion, challenge educators the most. Buckle up! Our destination is the behavior domain, and you never know who is going to be on the road with you for this ride!

FITNESS CHALLENGE

- Take time to explore the Ci3T website at ci3t.org to learn more about this amazing framework and how it can change you and/or your school professionally.
- Select one new instructional strategy to implement into your lesson plans that will actively engage students in the learning process.
- Make a list of your go-to instructional strategies. Assess if students are actively engaged in the learning process when utilizing your favorite strategies.

CHAPTER 4

THE ABCs OF SURVIVAL

THE Behavior DOMAIN

Every day, one of my sixth-grade students comes to school with an animal in tow—a turtle, snake, fish, or even a strange bug to show off to his peers. I meet with his mother and share that although I do not mind his love for animals, I prefer that he schedule and limit such visitors to our classroom because they are a distraction to learning. Her reply: "No need to worry about him bringing any more animals to class. His hamster is the only pet left to bring, and his gonads are so big he can't even walk, let alone survive show and tell." I thank her for her support.

Ah, my favorite domain! Why, you ask? You never know what animal or student behavior is going to show up in class each day. Student behavior is unpredictable for a variety of reasons: personal or homelife concerns, past traumatic experiences, mental instability, attention seeking, and avoidance of work, just to name a few. The list could go on and on, which is why classroom management is such a challenge. As Dr. Lane says, if you have ever tried on Spandex, it is obvious that one size does not fit all. This is also true for students and behavior, which supports the desperate need for a framework that clearly outlines what to do for students at all three levels of the pyramid as it relates to managing their behavior.

Having been an administrator for more than twenty years, I have structured the behavioral expectations in the schools in which I have served in a variety of ways; however, for many years, I was of the belief that teachers should have the autonomy to establish their own set of rules and expectations and handle discipline in a way that fits their personal belief systems. Today, I firmly believe administrators must implement a school-wide behavior plan so that every single teacher, staff member, student, parent, and community member knows the expectations, speaks the same language, and buys into the belief system.

Student behavior is one of the main reasons teachers are becoming burned out and leaving the profession. I was also in this situation and was ready to pursue another career, but I found a system that has alleviated the majority of my angst and has provided me with the stamina to remain in the profession I love and am so passionate about.

Ci3T very clearly supports the use of Positive Behavior Interventions and Supports (PBIS) as its framework for the management of student behavior. If you could see and hear me right now, you would see me doing a happy dance as I sing the praises of this wonderful program. PBIS changed my life as well as the lives of my staff members.

> I receive a call that assistance is needed in a kindergarten classroom. I make my way down the hallway to find a young lady at the front of the room mooning her class. Of course, she is getting all kinds of attention for this behavior from her peers, and the teacher is doing her very best to ignore the behavior. I make an announcement that I need a helper in the office and who might be available to help me. Of course, this caught the attention of my nearly naked friend, and she immediately volunteered. I accepted her request to help, and we exited the classroom with our clothes on, as a bonus. Attention is attention, dressed or undressed!

PBIS—A SHIFT TO THE POSITIVE

Positive Behavior Interventions and Supports is an evidence-based, three-tiered framework to address the behavioral needs of all students and will help them to remain clothed in your classroom![8] It was introduced by the Center on PBIS in 1998 and has a plethora of research to back up its credibility. It is a school-wide framework for behavioral expectations that are clearly defined and recommended by the Ci3T team. Positive behavior is reinforced, and all members at the school speak the same behavioral language.

Tier One focuses on a school-wide PBIS plan where all students have opportunities to be recognized for their positive behavior. Tier Two provides targeted interventions for students who struggle to be successful at Tier One. Tier Three provides the most intensive level of intervention. Administrators, school specialists, teachers, and, at

---

8   Positive Behavioral Interventions and Supports, pbis.org, accessed July 26, 2023.

times, the special education staff meet to create an individual plan for a student who demonstrates extreme behavioral needs. Tier Three does not automatically identify a student who comes from teacher referrals and extensive testing for special education services. However, the special education staff is a great resource for any intervention team.

The Center on PBIS is grounded in the values of comprehensive prevention, based on human-centered science, and implemented through collaborative partnerships, centered in equity, to improve social, emotional, behavioral, and academic outcomes.

The word that speaks to me the most in this definition is *prevention*. For years, I have worked from a reactive behavior system that caught students being naughty and assigned consequences. Today, we employ strategies to prevent the behavior from occurring in the first place with a purposeful effort to build students' social-emotional skills as well. Genius!

I will never forget the time I learned about PBIS. My school psychologist asked me the question:

"What do we do when a child cannot read or solve math equations?"

"We teach them," I asserted!

However, she then brought to my attention that when a child misbehaves, we often blame the child for the behavior and say things such as "You should know better."

The stance PBIS takes is that if children knew better, they would do better. It is our job to teach behavior just as we teach any other content area in the curriculum. PBIS is a positive, proactive, and preventative approach to student behavior rather than a punitive and reactive approach. It is a breath of fresh air and will change your perspective, outlook, and attitude in your school.

When schools respond to negative behaviors with consequences and punishments in isolation, the students do not learn the skills they need to change those behaviors. Obviously, there are times when students must be removed from classrooms or suspended from school. However, there must always be a teaching element coupled with the consequence so that the child can learn appropriate ways to respond to emotionally charged situations. If we do not teach them better skills, they will continue making the same mistakes.

The framework for PBIS is as follows:

1. Clearly defined behavioral expectations are agreed upon by staff and students for all areas of the school. Rules are generated for the following areas: classroom, hallway, bathroom, library, gym or physical education, bus lane, and cafeteria.
2. The expectations are taught to students and staff and followed with fidelity.
3. Students and staff are given opportunities to practice the behavior expectations.
4. Students and staff are rewarded for following expectations with a ticket, verbal praise, tangible prizes (such as M&Ms), and intangible prizes (such as getting to sit in the teacher's chair).
5. Behaviors such as classroom infractions, office discipline referrals, nurse visits, and attendance/tardies are tracked and monitored as a basis for improvement.

The first step in becoming a PBIS school is to identify three or four core values. One option is to consider the name of the school's mascot and use it as a starting point to brainstorm the core values. My school district's mascot is a bearcat. We chose to use the word CATS as our motto with the following four core values.

C Courage
A Attitude
T Take Responsibility
S Safe

Some school districts struggle to tie the name of the mascot to the core values, and that is fine. Many schools use the three words, Safe, Respectful, and Responsible, as their core values and simply add the picture of their mascot to the signage.

BEHAVIOR EXPECTATIONS AND SIGNAGE

The next step is to create school-wide behavioral expectations for all areas in your school. They should be linked to your motto, clearly defined, and published on a Behavior Matrix. Posters and signage highlighting the core values and behavior expectations should be hung about the school as visual cues as to how to behave. My school district invested in professional signage that serves as visual cues. We do not anticipate students stopping in the hallway to read a sign word-for-word, but they will see the signage and be reminded of what we value at our school and what the behavioral expectations are for them.

Once the signage is in place, it is time to teach the students the behavioral expectations. For the elementary level, I have the students rotate to all areas of the school (cafeteria, hallway, library, bus lane, bathrooms, playground) and attend a lesson outlining the expectations. For secondary students, we teach and review the expectations during a seminar class. We review the expectations weekly, especially in areas where we are seeing an increase in negative behavior. Next, we begin the process of reinforcing students who follow the expectations.

POSITIVE RECOGNITION

PBIS clearly promotes that students should be recognized for their positive behavior contributions. A concern about the implementation of PBIS is that students are awarded with tangible prizes when they follow the behavioral expectations. This could potentially cause them to be driven by extrinsic rather than intrinsic motivation. In other words, prizes could bribe students to behave when they should be motivated to behave by earning good grades. I do not buy into this notion. I often put tangible rewards in my teachers' mailboxes, anything from their favorite candy bar to a small gift card to a certificate to leave early for the day. I believe that there needs to be a balance between tangible and intangible rewards for behavior.

Students who struggle with significant behavioral concerns may need more tangible rewards written into a specific plan where others will not need any tangible rewards at all. However, PBIS is a systemic plan, and all students must receive some sort of positive feedback about their behavior. At my school district, I built an extensive list of prizes that are both tangible and intangible for our PBIS program. Over the years, I have evolved our prize list and added a variety of prizes and experiences students can earn through weekly, monthly, and quarterly drawings. For example, we have done a drawing to win a trip to the local animal shelter where our students read to the dogs and cats in residence. Our students learn about the center during a tour and give back to our community by interacting with the animals. There are so many ways to recognize and honor students for good behavior that teach them the importance of being good people and productive citizens. Bribery is illegal, but recognizing students and staff with tangible and intangible rewards is not bribery. It is thoughtful reinforcement of the expectations.

WE GET WHAT WE REINFORCE

Interestingly, teachers get what they reinforce in their classrooms. If you are a teacher who reprimands students regularly, then those attention-seeking students will pick up on that habit and do whatever it takes to get your attention in a negative way. Shift your mindset by recognizing well-behaved students, and the attention seekers will also pick up on this change. You might actually find that you and your students are happier. This does not mean that we ignore dangerous behaviors. Intervene when you must, but the overall atmosphere of your classroom must be positive in order for you to see a change in climate, culture, and student behavior. Doesn't maintaining a happy and healthy climate and culture in classrooms and schools sound more enjoyable than the alternative we have been enduring? Let's choose happy!

TICKETS VERSUS ELECTRONIC POINT SYSTEMS

There are two options for recognizing students in a tangible manner. Teachers can utilize actual tickets that are designed and pre-printed in advance, or they can utilize an electronic system, such as Class Dojo, that tracks who earns points throughout a day for positive behavior. At the elementary level, I recommend paper tickets because the students receive a tangible representation for positive behavior immediately. Older students can thrive on electronic systems that monitor and track their positive contributions to the school via a system.

Once a student has earned a ticket or electronic points, teachers are not to take them away should the student misbehave later in the day, no matter how tempted. We are building the self-esteem of our children, not tearing them down when they make a mistake.

We do not ignore misbehavior. We address it appropriately, but we do not take away tickets or points already earned. I have used both tickets and electronic recognition programs, and there are pros and cons to both. Tickets remind teachers to use specific praise when they hand the ticket to the child. It is easy to just award electronic points to students and forget to deliver the praise. The entire reason for using such systems is to use effort-based praise. If that does not occur, the system will not be successful. Tickets are cumbersome and can be difficult for students and teachers to track. Electronic systems track data for you and also tend to be more effective with secondary students who might see the tickets as juvenile. Your leadership team needs to decide what system is the best fit for your school.

If you choose to use tickets, have your staff devise a plan for how the tickets are going to be dispersed, signed, and collected. I have been in classrooms where a student earns a ticket and they pop out of their seats, looking for a pen or pencil to sign the ticket, and then make their way across the room, and deposit the ticket into a central collection jar, all the while disrupting instruction. If the system is disruptive to learning, it will not work. I would advise teachers to provide students with a pencil pouch at their desk. When they earn a ticket, they put it in their pouch, sign, and turn it in at a designated time.

PBIS is a data-driven system. Tracking who earns tickets or points is a great way to monitor student growth in the area of behavior and serves as a guide to behavioral interventions. We have learned that many of our well-behaved students earn fewer tickets or points than our students who struggle with behavior. When a naughty student is behaving appropriately, we are eager to award them tickets or points. However, those who are well behaved fly lower on the radar, so our data serves as a reminder that we must recognize all students. Some students will not care about the tickets or points, which is fine. Some of my students never turned in their tickets for prizes because they simply wanted to see how many they could earn in a year. Other students were not motivated by the tickets, yet they maintained excellent behavior. These students were already internally motivated. Then there are the Tier Three students who may not buy into the system at all. This is fine, too, but your team is going to have to devise an alternative plan that will motivate them with a more intensive and individualized recognition plan.

Similar to academics, our school assesses behavior and social-emotional skills just like we do for academic progress. There are a variety of behavior/social-emotional screeners available, but I use the SRSS-IE screener (Student Risk Screening Scale: Intrinsic and Extrinsic behaviors) offered free from the Ci3T website. This screener assesses the overall mental health of students and provides data that drives interventions. This screener should be done quarterly, and data should be shared and reviewed with staff. It takes very little time, less than thirty minutes, for teachers to complete this assessment, and it provides relevant data, making it well worth the time it takes to complete.

> *PBIS doesn't ignore problem behavior. Schools still use discipline,*
> *but punishment isn't the focus. Instead, the focus is on teaching*
> *expectations, preventing problems, and using logical consequences.*

—WWW.UNDERSTOOD.ORG, ANDREW M. I. LEE

Templates for all PBIS materials needed to develop a system-wide PBIS program can be found on ci3t.org, but there are many other PBIS resources available to you. Here is the list of my team's go-to for PBIS materials.

- *Supporting Behavior for School Success*, Kathleen Lane, PhD
- pbis.org

- Safe and Civil Schools, *CHAMPS*, Randy Sprick, PhD
- Safeandcivilschools.com
- Zones of Regulation
- Restorative Justice

It is the end of a busy day. A teacher brings a large group of students back to the office because they threw snowballs at one another in the bus lane. All but one of the students seem to feel remorseful about the situation. He begins to mimic my reprimand and make funny faces behind my back. I ask him to wait in my office so that I can address him alone. From my office, I hear furniture being moved. This child then yells that he is going to jump out of the window. I ignore him. It is a one-story building. Should he "jump," the damage will be minimal, and I am certain he is bluffing. The next thing I know, this child is standing in front of me. Not only did he jump, but he ran back into the building and directly to me!

It seems as if the naughty kids are never absent. In fact, they almost always win the Perfect Attendance award at the conclusion of each quarter! They are going to be in school, so we must have classroom management plans in place that address all behaviors, including threatening to jump out of a window! The book, *CHAMPS: A Proactive and Positive Approach to Classroom Management*, is another amazing resource I have used that offers teachers practical, positive, and effective strategies to set up a successful classroom as it relates to classroom management.

CHAMPS: A PROACTIVE AND POSITIVE APPROACH TO CLASSROOM MANAGEMENT

Jessica Sprick, Dr. Randy Sprick, Jacob Edwards, and Cristy Coughlin

Classroom management is a journey not a destination.

—RANDY SPRICK

CHAMPS, which we explored in the previous chapter in terms of instructional design, is also rich in ideas for how to foster a positive and proactive classroom, thus making both students and teachers healthier and happier and hopefully in the classroom for years to come.

Dr. Sprick and his team take a very positive and proactive (PBIS) stance with student discipline and back up their beliefs with an amazing amount of research. The stance they take regarding student behavior is that misbehavior is not the result of a poor student, but the result of a poor behavior system. Also, punitive consequences that offer no sort of rehabilitation around the challenging behavior are ineffective.

Dr. Sprick asserts that highly effective teachers have classroom management plans that include the following elements:

- High expectations for student success
- Positive relationships with students
- Consistent, predictable classroom routines
- Students are taught how to behave successfully
- Students are provided with frequent, positive feedback
- Misbehavior is corrected in a calm, consistent, and logical manner[9]

---

9   Randy S. Sprick and Keba Baldwin, *CHAMPS: A Proactive and Positive Approach to Classroom Management* (Eugene, OR: Pacific Northwest Publishing, 2009).

Behavior, no matter how challenging, can be changed.

—RANDY SPRICK

Students misbehave in school for a variety of reasons. If the teacher has not taught the expectations, the students may not know them. The students do not have the skills to behave appropriately, or the students love attention whether it be positive or negative. If the teacher spends more time calling out students for misbehavior, the attention-seeking child will pick up on this habit and turn up the volume to fulfill their need for attention. Finally, some students have learned that if they misbehave, it gets them out of doing the academic task at hand. They misbehave as a way to avoid doing the work. It is important to identify what motivates a child's negative behavior in order to change the behavior for the better.

Students and educators have the capacity to be "CHAMPS" in the classroom. Behavior is learned, so it can be taught, no matter how challenging. Dr. Sprick encourages educators to not be fearful of challenging student behavior but to look at behavior as a puzzle to be solved. In the book, *CHAMPS,* the authors offer strategies or pieces to the puzzle to utilize in order to successfully manage student behavior.

A successful classroom is created around the variables of which teachers have control and comprise the following elements from the acronym, *STOIC.*

S: Structure: Educators have control over the physical structure of the classroom. The physical setting alone can set the tone for the classroom environment. The strategies and quality of instruction are included in the category of structure as well. Student engagement in instruction decreases poor behavior choices. The bottom line is to arrange the classroom in a way that is conducive to positive and respectful behavior.

Items to consider regarding *STRUCTURE* are as follows:

- Classroom guidelines, rules, and procedures are in place and posted.
- Assigned seats.
- Does the teacher wish to provide flexible seating, such as beanbags, yoga balls, stools, pillows, recliner chair, or other options? (Personally, I cannot handle the up and down movement of yoga balls, so be cautious in finding options for your students that work for you.)
- The physical arrangement of desks or tables is taken into consideration. What is the teacher's tolerance for student conversation? Should desks be in rows or side-by-side, groups of four or in a U shape? Again, choose arrangements that you as the teacher can tolerate.
- Do students have visual access to pertinent instructional materials, such as whiteboards and interactive boards? Can the teacher see all the students in a manner to supervise them effectively?
- Student work should be posted with pride giving students a sense of ownership and relevance in the classroom. I would also add that the work that is posted is not all perfect or "A" work. Student work that exemplifies great effort should always be included if not prioritized.

T: Teach: Students must understand the behavioral expectations in order to abide by them. The expectations must be explicitly taught prior to each activity, lesson, transition time, and independent or cooperative activity. The teacher can model expected behavior or have students model and practice behavioral expectations for activities as well, thus ensuring understanding.

O: Observe: The teacher must be actively engaged while students work. Circulating the classroom while students work, offering feedback, and intervening as necessary to clarify the expectations are recommended. Data from such observations can also serve as valuable information about student learning and behavior.

I: Interact Positively: The climate of the classroom is dependent upon the teacher's capacity to build healthy relationships with students. Maintaining a classroom climate with a focus on students' positive contributions will greatly enhance the overall classroom climate. Praise for students' work delivered in a manner that highlights students' effort rather than innate abilities is recommended. Implementing positive responses to correct behaviors such as verbal praise, tokens, treats, or rewards is another way to build relationships and set a positive tone in a classroom.

Positive interactions with students build relationships, and healthy relationships between students and teachers are the foundation for a positive classroom climate. Someone once told me that students will not work for a teacher they do not like, and during my tenure, I have found this fact to be painfully true. The teacher is the adult and is charged with setting the tone in the classroom. We can all learn content in order to teach it, but interpersonal skills are a little trickier and take effort, especially if it is not an area of strength.

RELATIONSHIPS

If students are going to work harder for a teacher they care about, then how can teachers go about building such relationships?

- You get what you reinforce. If you wish to benefit from healthy relationships with students, then you must reinforce the positive behaviors and contributions of students. An average classroom should have a ratio of three positive interactions with a student to every one corrective statement. Corrective statements are not demeaning or belittling. They are redirections done in a manner that preserves a student's dignity and treats them with respect. A 3:1 ratio is the bare minimum for such interactions. Truly, a 5:1 or up to a 9:1 ratio of positive to corrective statements is probably more accurate for today's students since they need more support than they have in the past. Some students are starved for attention; overload them with positive observations, and build those relationships one by one.

- Meet and Greet: Welcome your students to your classroom each and every day. Know their names, and offer sincere praise whenever possible by noticing differences in their appearance, outfits, new shoes, or just that they have a smile on their face. It will make a difference.

- Show an interest in their work, habits, hobbies, and culture. Surveys, lunch meetings, and having students share about their background with you and/or the class are great ways to connect and build relationships with them.

- Share your habits, hobbies, interests, strengths, and challenges with students. It may make you feel vulnerable, but it will open the lines of communication and build trust between all parties.

- Students who struggle with behavior may be fearful to engage in a relationship with teachers for fear that they have ruined the relationship. This is the sort of student to go above and beyond with as it relates to building a relationship. A healthy relationship is the foundation for the process of improving behavior.

C: Correct Fluently: Teachers must address inappropriate behavior; however, how this is done impacts the climate either positively or negatively. Also, the focus in the classroom must rely more heavily on positive student behavior rather than negative student behavior. No matter how severe a situation, a student's dignity must always be protected. Students and teachers must be treated with respect, and the adults set the tone by modeling such respect. Yelling and demeaning misbehaving students damage relationships, the classroom climate, and the self-esteem of students. Corrections should be brief, delivered in a calm and respectful manner, consistent, and delivered privately when possible.

I am meeting and greeting students for the day when a student taps me on the shoulder. She is a new student, and today is her first day of school. She is wearing what looks like a ball gown with a fur stole wrapped around her shoulders. Her face is painted with makeup as if she is the Mary Kay consultant of the year, and she is dripping in costume jewelry. The icing on the cake; she is wearing a "diamond" studded tiara. Sound the trumpets; the Queen has arrived!

Teachers must prepare to work with students from all walks of life, including those who quite possibly descended from a Royal Family. When I was a teacher, I would spend my summers planning the annual theme for my classroom, thinking about how I was going to tweak the décor, designing bulletin boards, and planning how to begin lessons and units, all of which are critically important. However, it is equally important to outline an effective classroom management plan.

CLASSROOM MANAGEMENT PLAN

A teacher's classroom management plan incorporates expectations from both the school's Guidelines for Success and the classroom rules. Guidelines for Success highlight aspirations where rules state the basic behavioral requirements aligned with these aspirations. In a previous example, I noted how my school chose the word CATS for our motto. This motto also serves as our Guidelines for Success in that we highlight the words Courage, Positive Attitude, Take Responsibility, and Safety as our global aspirations. Teachers' classroom management plans and rules should mirror the school-wide plan.

Words and phrases that are highly effective for Guidelines for Success are as follows:

- Give Your Best
- Persevere
- Demonstrate Integrity
- Be Kind
- Cooperate
- Respect
- Be Curious
- Show Effort
- Growth Mindset
- Have a Positive Attitude

CLASSROOM RULES

Classroom rules state the behavioral requirements for a classroom within a school. Some teachers like to include students in the process of developing the classroom rules. Such involvement fosters a sense of ownership of the rules by the students. Other teachers prefer to develop their own rules and teach them directly to the students. I prefer a combination of these approaches. I want to encourage student buy-in and ownership of the rules, while at the same time, I want the rules to reflect my needs as the teacher to run a successful classroom. Most importantly, the rules must be implemented on the first day of school in order to provide students with structure and consistency and to avoid the development of any poor habits. No matter if students are involved in the creation of the rules, they should be positive, proactive, clear, and the best fit for the teacher and students. There should only be three to five classroom rules, and they should always be stated in a positive framework such as "Treat Everyone with Respect" versus "No Hitting." There are several items teachers should review and evaluate when devising their classroom management plan, and they are as follows:

- How many students are on the roster?
- What are the demographics of the roster?
- Are there any specific behavioral needs of students on the roster?
- Are there any specific familial concerns or needs, such as custody cases or legal concerns for students on the roster?
- Have any of the students experienced trauma?
- How many students have special education needs?
- Who is new to the school?
- Review students' academic and social-emotional data along with information in their cumulative records.

- MOST IMPORTANT: How much noise and movement can I tolerate in order to run an effective and efficient classroom?

The classroom rules must take into consideration all the needs of the students and the teacher for it to be effective.

Classroom rules are a great starting point to a successful school year; however, the savvy teacher realizes that students must not only understand the rules but also see value in behaving responsibly. Establishing a positive and proactive approach to student management will feed students with the praise needed to acquire value in good behavior.

Delivering praise is most definitely an art and, if done correctly, can be extremely powerful. Helpful hints for utilizing praise effectively are as follows:

- Feedback must be true and accurate. When working hard to build a positive classroom, it can be easy to misuse or overuse praise. The praise should be specific to the child and linked to something they specifically did in order for it to be meaningful.
- Avoid the use of generic words and phrases, such as "Good Job" or "Excellent." Be specific with praise highlighting what the student did that pleased you. For example, "Your effort on this assignment is impressive; thank you for your hard work."
- Growth Mindset praise: Be so careful not to praise students based on their innate talents or abilities, such as "You are brilliant!" or "You are such a gifted musician." This sort of praise sends the message to your students that you have to be smart or talented in order to achieve greatness. We have learned from Carol Dweck that the brain is a muscle and, with practice, can learn anything. Praise must be linked to student effort.

- Praise should be age appropriate and performed in a manner that does not embarrass the student. Get to know your students, and learn how they prefer to be recognized. Some may prefer private affirmation where others enjoy being the sage on the stage. Middle-school students are very challenging to praise, and your efforts may backfire if they become embarrassed even if they do feel flattered. Use a quiet voice, be brief in your comments, be businesslike, and avoid hanging around after the praise for affirmation. Feel out your students, and deliver praise that suits their needs.
- Praise should be used in an immediate fashion. This should be easy since you are looking for positive behaviors. Deliver it in a timely fashion.
- Use praise that is natural to you in order for it to be sincere.

Along with the praise, teachers must implement what Dr. Sprick terms "Pleasant Consequences" for appropriate actions. Praise coupled with a tangible item, such as a ticket, token, or point system, is the recipe for success. There are several options for such a system, and they are as follows.

PLEASANT CONSEQUENCES

Students and staff deserve and enjoy being recognized for their positive contributions to the school. The common complaint is that students should do what they are supposed to do without extrinsic rewards. I wholeheartedly disagree. Think about how you feel when someone leaves a positive note in your mailbox, or reaches out by phone to thank you for your efforts, or delivers a soft drink to your door won from a drawing. It feels good. Please, get past this, and set your school and classroom up for success by rewarding, recognizing, and celebrating all members of your community, including parent volunteers.

> *A bus driver schedules a time to meet with me. Upon his arrival, he informs me that he would like to bring his gun on his morning route. With alarm, I inquire as to why in the world he would need a rifle to drive his bus route? His response: "There is an amazing buck on that route!" My response: "That is a really bad idea," with thoughts of him pulling the bus over, shooting the buck in front of the kids, and then having the children haul the carcass back to the bus. Bad idea!*

Although a buck would be an amazing prize, it is not the sort of prize I am referring to as it relates to positive behavior strategies, students, and schools. There are a number of systems that provide administrators with options to recognize and honor staff and students.

Ticket System: Teachers dispense tickets to students who demonstrate positive behaviors aligned to the school's Guidelines or Classroom Rules. Tickets are accompanied with verbal praise highlighting the student's effort, grit, or perseverance.

GUIDELINES FOR TICKET REINFORCEMENT SYSTEMS

1. Names for such tickets can be created and associated with a school or mascot such as Lottery Tickets, Bearcat Bucks, Mustang Money, Bulldog Bucks, or Panther Paws.

2. It is critical to note that once a student has received a ticket, the teacher cannot take it away should the child misbehave later in the day. The entire point of using such a system is to build students' character and self-esteem. Taking tickets away with a verbal reprimand will sabotage this sort of plan.

3. Teachers must devise a system for handing out, signing, and submitting tickets so that instruction is not interrupted by the use of positive reinforcement with tickets. Teachers in my schools have made copies of tickets, whole-punched them, and hung them on their lanyards with a key ring so that they have easy access to them. When a student behaves well, the teacher simply tears off a ticket, praises the student, and delivers the ticket to the student. Once the student earns a ticket, there must be a system for signing and submitting it in a manner that does not disrupt the learning process. For instance, a teacher who prefers to seat students in groups might place a small bucket in the center of the grouping for students to sign and place tickets in a timely fashion. Some teachers prefer to provide pencil pouches to students. Students receive a ticket, sign it, and place it in the pouch with no disruption to learning. I would not recommend having a central location for tickets where students have to get up and walk across the room to turn in a ticket during instruction. At the end of the school day, the teacher will conduct a roll call where students report the number of tickets they earned during the day. Students then submit signed tickets to the teacher in order to be placed into a drawing for daily, weekly, or monthly prizes. Teachers track the number of tickets students earn daily in an effort to monitor student behavior. This system assists teachers in assuring that all

students are being recognized for their positive contributions to the classroom as well as identifying which students are not earning tickets and what can be done to improve their behavior. There will be some teachers who express concern that some students are not motivated by the tickets. This is TRUE! Some students do not need tangible reinforcement to behave but continue to include them in the process. They do deserve the praise, and although they may not act as if the tickets are important, that really might not be the case. I once learned that a student took every ticket home rather than entering them into school or classroom drawings. She hung them on the wall of her bedroom as a trophy of her good behavior. School personnel thought she did not care when she simply cared in her own way. I have also had students collect tickets throughout the entire school year to see how many they could earn. With tickets comes praise; pass them out by the bundles!

Class Dojo: Class Dojo is a system where students can earn points for good behavior electronically.

1. The student selects a computer Dojo to represent themselves.
2. The teacher then assigns points to the Dojo or student when rules and guidelines are followed. The system tallies the points and tracks student data, which is a bonus for teachers.
3. One downside to this system is that it allows teachers to take points away from students if they misbehave. I do not support this practice due to the damage such an action can have on teacher and student relationships.

4. Another downfall to this system has to do with the delivery of praise that is specific to student effort, grit, and perseverance. When a teacher hand delivers a ticket, it is easy to remember to include the praise. However, when adding points to a computer system, the teacher might have to step away from students or award the points when not teaching, making the delivery of praise less reliable. However, at the very least, this system sets up a classroom to recognize students for good behavior, which is key to a successful classroom climate and culture. Class Dojo is best used with elementary students. There are other similar systems that have computer icons more appropriate for middle-school-aged students such as the following.

5 STAR Point System: This positive reinforcement system is unique in that students' school badges are scanned by teachers' phones, iPads, or even scanners purchased through the company when they earn points or praise for positive behavior.

1. Students earn points for being on time to class, participating appropriately, finishing their work, or simply following the school's guidelines or classroom rules.

2. Student Council members or surveys could be used to seek input from students about how and what constitutes earning points as well as what sorts of prizes or incentives would best motivate them to behave. Some schools have used this system in a manner that students have to earn a certain number of points to attend athletic events, to be eligible to participate in extracurricular activities, or school dances.

3. Be certain to set students up for success by providing some easy ways to earn points. Students will not buy into a system they feel is impossible to be successful.

4. 5 Star has options for both elementary and secondary settings, but I have used it only at my secondary level.

ECONOMIC SYSTEM

Many schools opt to coin their positive behavior recognition program in a monetary style. Students earn "Dollars" or "Coins" for their healthy contributions to their school and for personal accomplishments. Students can monitor and track their money with a checking and/or savings account and can then spend their earnings in a school store on a weekly or monthly basis. The store can offer students both tangible and intangible shopping options, which will be detailed later in the chapter.

PROGRAM VARIETY

In my opinion, it is more effective to use a different reinforcement system at the elementary level from what is used at the secondary level. Having a novice program for students to adjust to at the secondary level is motivating to students. Also, utilizing praise with secondary students can be tricky. It has been my experience that the older students do not react to tangible tickets as well as the younger students. Some of them are embarrassed by the praise, even though they need it, so educators have to be tricky in its delivery. Scanning their badges and delivering praise in a discreet style have been more effective in my schools.

HUNDREDS CHART

This is an easy, yet highly motivational, way to recognize students and staff. Design a chart that has one hundred boxes (ten rows and ten columns). The size of the chart needs to be large enough so that students and staff can sign their names inside of one of the boxes. These charts can be used in classrooms for students or in the teachers' workroom for staff and PTO recognition. A teacher or administrator simply acknowledges an individual with specific praise and invites that individual to select a box to sign on the chart in recognition of their positive contributions. Here is where the fun begins. When an entire row or column is filled, everyone on that row gets a prize of some sort. When the entire one hundred boxes have been signed, a class or staff party has been earned.

MYSTERY BEHAVIOR OF THE DAY

Each morning, the teacher writes a behavior on a sheet of paper and puts it into a sealed envelope. She reminds the students throughout the day that she is keeping an eye on them as it relates to this mystery behavior. The teacher should keep track of students who exemplify this behavior, and then, at the end of the day, a student unseals the envelope and reveals the mystery behavior. The teacher can then recognize students who followed the expectations and exemplified the mystery behavior.

GIFT BOXES

Purchase several small gift boxes, and place a magnetic strip on the bottom of them. Each morning, fill the box with small trinkets, candies, or tickets, and stick them to the whiteboard. When the teacher notices a student going above and beyond, call the child's name to go to the board and select one of the gifts. The child then returns the gift box to the teacher's desk to be refilled for the next lucky winner.

PRIZE PATROL

I am still convinced that one day, the prize patrol will ring my doorbell; however, while I wait for their arrival, I will brainstorm ideas for potential prizes for students and staff. Prizes do not have to cost money and do not have to be tangible. The prizes are a way to recognize, thank, and reinforce the desired behaviors. Following is a list of ideas that I continue to add to over the years to keep prizes fresh and desirable for students and staff.

STUDENT PRIZES

- Unique pens, pencils, erasers, sticky notes, crayons, markers, colored pencils
- Homework pass
- Decorate a ceiling tile in the school
- Drop the lowest grade
- Drop one tardy
- Additional computer time
- Extra recess or break time
- Park in the principal's spot
- Plan a cafeteria meal with the cook
- Bake with the cafeteria cook
- Lead the Pledge of Allegiance for the school
- Share a joke of the day with the school
- Time to work on a class puzzle
- Lego time

- Play a game with teacher, principal, or superintendent
- Read a story to a younger grade
- Be an assistant in the day care
- Take a ride with the SRO and learn about the patrol car
- Use the teacher's chair for the day
- Name a hallway (monthly activity)
- Name the tables in the lunchroom
- Be a teacher's assistant
- Be a guest on the weekly newscast
- Bring a stuffed animal for a day
- Choose a movie for the lunchroom
- Chew gum in class
- Design and decorate a bulletin board
- Prom tickets
- Prom meal
- Concession stand coupons
- Ticket to an athletic event
- VIP seating at games
- Go to lunch first or early
- $5 gift cards (Sonic, Dollar General, McDonald's, etc.)
- Early release (fifteen minutes) from school
- Movie tickets
- Lunch brought to school (McDonald's, pizza, etc.)
- Lunch with teacher, principal, or superintendent
- Sky Zone pass
- Candy or food items
- School spirit wear
- Bowling passes
- Free yearbook
- Donate $5 to a charity of choice

- Laptop stickers
- Mystery prize bag
- Free book at book fair
- Fidgets or sensory items
- Highlight a book of the month from the library
- Trip to local shelter to read to the animals (multiple students can win this award)
- Trip to local rescue mission to deliver donations (multiple students can win this award)
- Trip to local soup kitchen to serve a meal (multiple students can win this award)
- Ice cream at lunch
- Choose a theme day for the school (favorite team jersey day, etc.)
- Class popcorn party
- Assist custodian
- Assist with morning announcements over the public address (PA) system
- Classroom aide
- Featured on a school-wide recognition bulletin board
- Teacher helper for the day
- First in line to lunch
- Borrow principal's chair for the day
- Choose music for the class to enjoy
- Choose game for recess or physical education class
- Choose class exercise break
- Draw on white or electronic board
- Tickets to the zoo
- Earn a trophy, certificate, medal, or ribbon
- Extra credit

- Lunch outdoors
- Have a special lunch with a friend
- Private lesson with music, art, computer, or specialty teacher
- Name on scrolling marquee with special message
- Read a book to the class
- Extra recess
- Art supplies
- Sit at teacher's desk
- Select a place to sit for the day
- Choose a class job for the week
- Earn a "Happy Postcard" to be sent to parents
- Lunch with local or high school athletes
- Positive phone call to home from teacher
- Design a class bulletin board
- Walk with a teacher during lunch
- Make a trip to the treasure box, and select a small prize (stickers, key chains, temporary tattoos, yo-yo, bubbles, erasers, pencil toppers, etc.)
- Take care of a class animal, or take it home during a school break
- Work in the lunchroom
- Do half of an assignment, or receive a free homework pass
- Coloring book/pencils
- Physical fitness item (jump rope, frisbee, basketball, football, Hula-Hoop, etc.)
- Listen to music with headphones
- Operate the remote for a teacher presentation
- Teach the class a favorite game
- Dedicate a new book to the school library in your name
- Make deliveries to the school office

- Take photo with the school mascot
- Wear a crazy hat
- Wear slippers or pajamas for a day
- Put up or take down the flag for the day
- Field trip
- Lunch at a local park

STAFF PRIZES

- Arrive thirty minutes late
- Leave thirty minutes early
- Jeans for a day
- Catered lunch
- Administration covers a class period
- Classroom supplies
- Gas cards
- Books
- Flowers or a plant
- Donation to charity
- Class photo in a frame
- Candy
- Ice cream
- $10 gift cards (Barnes and Noble, Casey's, Sonic, McDonald's, Bath and Body Works, Target, Starbucks, etc.)
- Favorite coffee or tea treat
- Breakfast treat
- Donuts for the class
- Comfortable chair at staff meeting
- Movie tickets
- Concession stand coupons

- School spirit wear
- School supplies
- Off-campus lunch with coverage
- Massage
- Class popcorn party
- Alumni gear
- Special parking spot
- Name on scrolling marquee with special message
- Insulated tumbler
- Gourmet cookie or cupcake
- Shout out on social media, morning announcements, or school newsletter
- Framed photo with the school mascot
- Become a member of the Hall of Fame
- Cooking lesson at a local market
- Fancy chocolate bars
- Fun socks

UNIVERSAL ATTENTION SIGNAL

It is interesting to attend professional conferences led by non-educators. The speakers always seem to struggle to get the attention of the attendees to start the presentation. Dr. Sprick recommends adopting a school-wide attention signal, and I have found this strategy to be highly effective. The signal should be able to be utilized in any setting. Many educators turn lights on and off to gain their students' attention, but on a field trip, there will not be a light switch. The most effective signal I have used in my schools is as follows: I raise my hand and state, "May I have your attention, please?" The students see my hand go up in the air as a cue and immediately respond by raising their own hands and becoming quiet. Every teacher in my school utilizes this same approach to create a more unified system. The same signal is used in every part of the school and on field trips, in the lunchroom, on bus rides, and even in PTO meetings. Our entire community uses this signal, and it is a quiet and respectful way in which to grab the attention of your audience, which adds to the positive climate and culture in the classroom and school.

BELL TO BELL

The most effective strategy to positive behavior management is to keep the students engaged in learning from bell to bell. If teachers allow for unstructured time, the students will find creative ways to fill it and most likely in ways that are not enjoyable for the teacher. Having a quick activity planned for students the minute they arrive to class gives students a task to attend to as well as an expectation to follow. The bell work, so to say, should be something that the students can complete on their own so that the teacher can welcome students to class and be attentive during the transition period. Similarly, when students notice that the end of the period is looming, they become antsy. Provide them with what is called an Exit Ticket for the period. This is an exercise that has them respond to something that was taught during the lesson that day. They must answer the question and hand the teacher the response on their way out the door. Students simply do not have enough time to be off task, and the teacher enjoys minimal behavioral challenges.

TRANSITION PERIODS

Transition periods offer students a bit of freedom and, if not structured, can result in behavioral problems. Teachers need to plan how they expect students to both enter and exit their classrooms. How do they manage their supplies? Do they use cubbies in the classroom or lockers in the hallways? How much time do the students need to transition? Will they change groups during instruction? Do they need time to clean up for the day, and what does that look like? Every moment counts, and the more structured the moments, the better the school day.

VOICE LEVELS

Voice levels should be utilized school-wide in order to promote consistency across all areas of the building. My school utilizes signage in all areas of the school to remind students of the expected voice levels. We use the following scale as a guide to the level of noise allowed at all times in the school:

0 Silent
1 Whisper
2 Speaking
3 Presenting
4 Outside

There are a variety of options for voice level descriptions and signage, and some are more elementary than secondary. However, it is critical that all members of the community clearly understand the voice level expectations. One of my teachers uses a battery-operated light on her Voice Level Chart and lights the expected level as a visual cue when students are working. Genius!

MISBEHAVIOR

So what do teachers do when students misbehave? A common misconception with any positive behavior system is that some will automatically assume that there are no consequences to the negative behaviors. This could not be further from the truth. The difference is in how the consequences are delivered and what the expectations are moving forward.

A student arrives at the office with a disciplinary referral in hand. He hit a fellow student in the head with a clipboard. I realize that this same child has been in the office several times this week for the exact same reason. I learn this child carries a clipboard with a behavior plan attached so that teachers can assess his behavior in all settings. This is ironic. His behavior has become more problematic due to a clipboard with his improvement plan attached. Time to think of a new strategy. Maybe a folder?

Teachers have choices when delivering consequences for students and more so than just choosing between a clipboard and a folder! However, the common factor regarding all consequences is that teaching the student to behave better should always be a factor in the equation.

CONSEQUENCE TIPS

- Do not get angry. No matter how upsetting a student's behavior may be, do not let it show. Maintain your dignity at all times. Occasionally, all of us will blow a gasket, but that cannot be the go-to response to naughty behavior. Students, all people in general, do not like being yelled at, belittled, and demeaned, especially in front of peers. Take some deep breaths, step away, say a prayer, or do whatever it takes, but maintain your composure.

- Praise a student who is demonstrating appropriate behavior in front of someone who is misbehaving. Do not use sarcasm, but sincerely thank those who are behaving, and some of the less disruptive behaviors can be corrected without having said anything to the offender. They will be motivated to earn your praise next!

- Proximity: Position yourself and teach from an area near a misbehaving student. Your presence alone may deter such behavior.

- Compliment a student who is misbehaving about something else or about their character in order to distract the student from misbehaving. For example, "John, can you share how your hard work on your last project made a difference in your grade?" or, "Kaitlyn, will you give the class a couple of tips about how to complete this activity since your focus is usually spot on?"

- Use humor to redirect students rather than a punitive approach.

- Approach a student, and whisper a constructive suggestion, and then thank the child and walk away immediately. Very little attention should be given to the naughty behavior. Then, when the student begins to exhibit positive behavior, swoop in and compliment them immediately, thus reinforcing the expectations.

- Talk privately with a student if behaviors persist. Perhaps, the teacher and the student can set a behavior goal together and monitor the behavior reinforcing when the student performs well. It is best to do this at a time when the other students do not recognize that one of their peers is in trouble or having to talk to the teacher.

- Check In, Check Out: If a student is struggling with behavior in a class, select an adult who has a healthy relationship with the student to check in with the student in the morning and discuss behavior goals for the school day. At the end of the day, the student returns to the adult and reports how the day went behaviorally. The student should carry a form to class that allows the teacher and the student to reflect and assess behavior throughout the day, or the student may forget how the day actually went for them. Be careful NOT to only report the negative behaviors on such a form. Think how you would feel if your principal completed a form about you daily that only highlights what you did wrong. Schools so often use this approach, and it can be very damaging. Of course, significant concerns can and should be noted, but I never assign a zero or a frown face to students; it is too damaging to their self-esteem.

- Create a space in your classroom where students can go if they are feeling anxious or upset. They are still in the classroom listening to instruction, but they are in a space in which they can relax and breathe for a minute.

- Buddy Classroom: If a child is too disruptive to remain in class, the teacher should have a pre-arranged plan with a colleague that this student can go to their classroom for an assigned period of time to de-escalate and then return to class.
- Provide a misbehaving student with a choice in order to distract them from the defiant behavior.
- Keep a chart or a timer, and track the number of times a student disrupts class. The child can then owe the teacher that same amount of time from a preferred task in an effort to help them recognize their behavior and correct it.
- Restitution: The student has to clean up the mess they made or find an appropriate way to apologize for their behavior in an effort to make things right.
- Teach and practice the appropriate behavior together with the child. This effort will also improve the relationship between the teacher and the student.
- Create a behavior plan with the student.
- Response Cost: Although this is not my favorite behavior management method, all students respond differently, and teachers need an arsenal of tools in their kits. In this model, a student might start a day with a certain number of points or tickets and has them taken away when they misbehave. Be careful not to damage a student's self-esteem when using this method. The teacher also does not want to damage the relationship with the student when taking away points or tickets, either, which is why I typically avoid this method unless all else has failed.

> *A fourth-grade teacher stops by my office to share a concern. She tells me she allows her students to give her a hug, high five, or wave each morning as they arrive at her classroom. The problem is that one of the boys always chooses a hug and lingers a bit too long with his head nestled in her chest region. I manage to hide a smile while I instruct her to not allow this child the option of a hug. Problem solved. She says, "It's your son!" Blushing with embarrassment, I assure her I will take care of it immediately.*

My son certainly had a choice in that situation, and he was definitely making the most of it, but teachers can also utilize the strategy of providing choices to manage student behaviors to their benefit as well. One system that prioritizes classroom management around the idea of choice is Love and Logic.

TEACHING WITH LOVE AND LOGIC[10]

You want your students to know that making it through a tough situation is always an option.

You can't make people angry and sell them something at the same time.

The easiest student to boss around is one who believes that the teacher is reasonable and takes control only when necessary.

—JIM FAY

---

10   Jim Fay and Charles Fay, *Teaching with Love and Logic: Taking Control of the Classroom* (Golden, CO: Love & Logic Institute, Incorporated, 2016).

I was nine months pregnant when I attended a Love and Logic seminar. The speaker was Jim Fay, one of the founders of the Love and Logic philosophy for parenting and teaching. Just a few minutes into the presentation, he had me hooked as well as laughing so hard I thought I might go into labor. Unfortunately, I soon learned that it was going to take a *lot* more than a good laugh to finally go into labor, but that is beside the point. I decided right then and there that this was the behavior management philosophy I was going to use with my students, my own children, and quite possibly with my husband when his behavior is questionable.

Love and Logic is not a new philosophy. I consider it tried and true. There are many elements of this behavior management system that I have found to be not only highly effective with children, but they preserve adult sanity as well. One reason Love and Logic resonates with me is its positive and proactive approach with students that fosters healthy relationships between teachers and students. However, Love and Logic also provides strategies to teachers to assist them to remain calm and strategies to students that teach them to think for themselves, solve their own problems, and improve their own behavior: questions and choices.

Children have little control over their day-to-day lives. At home, they respond to parental directives, and at school, they are responsible to follow the requests made by teachers, administrators, and coaches, leaving little time for them to develop any autonomy or control over their own lives. For students who struggle to regulate their own emotions due to stress, traumatic experiences, or a number of other variables, including an international pandemic, having little control is problematic because control is what makes them feel secure. Students who need to feel in control will find ways to do so; hence, teachers need to provide such opportunities on their terms, not the students' terms.

Control through questions and choices is a gift you can give to students that empowers them to be in charge of their own decisions, which, in turn, teaches them that they can solve their own problems and do not rely on adult directives. Love and Logic is not a proponent of the traditional model of classroom management where teachers post the rules and alongside those rules are the consequences. In this model, teachers inform students of the rules and punish the students when rules are broken, thus breaking down relationships between students and educators. To compound the ineffectiveness of this model, students do not learn to think for themselves or gain the confidence that they can solve their own problems. They learn that adults have to think and problem solve for them. In this model, it is the teacher who is doing all the thinking, which is exhausting. Let's change this!

> It is 9:15 a.m. I am visiting with my secretary when one of my kindergarten students walks into the office with her coat and backpack in tow. She looks me straight in the eye and says, "I am done for the day and am going home." I remind her that it is early in the day and that her teacher has wonderful activities planned for her and her friends. She takes a seat in the office, crosses her arms, and says, "Call my mom, or I'm walking." This could be a long day for both of us.

Clearly, this student is seeking control of her environment, so let's talk about some successful strategies that will entice such a child to remain at school while, at the same time, building her capacity to make successful decisions as it relates to her behavior.

In a Love and Logic classroom, the control between teacher and student is shared. The first step in creating such a climate is for teachers to phrase directives in a way that implies that the students have partial control over the situation. Jim Fay coins this practice as turning your directives from "garbage to gold." The following are a few examples of how to do this taken directly from his book.[11]

GARBAGE TO GOLD

GARBAGE STATEMENTS	GOLD STATEMENTS
I'm not going to line students up for recess until everyone is quiet.	I'll line students up for recess as soon as we are quiet.
Don't sharpen your pencil while I am teaching.	I allow students to sharpen their pencils when I am not teaching or giving directions.
You can't go to the restroom until I finish giving directions.	Feel free to use the restroom when I am not giving directions.
Don't bother your neighbors.	You're welcome to stay in class as long as you and others are not bothered.
Turn in your assignment on time or you will receive a lower grade.	I give full credit for work that is turned in on time.
Raise your hand if you wish to talk to me.	I listen to students who raise their hands.
Don't talk to me in that tone of voice.	I will listen to you when your voice sounds like mine.

What a difference such a small change in delivery will make in your classroom! The aforementioned statements give the students the feeling that they are in charge of their behaviors rather than having to

---

11   Jim Fay, *Teaching with Love and Logic* (New York: Love & Logic, 2016).

respond to a teacher who barks directives all day. Instantly, the climate and culture in your classroom will shift for the better. I concentrate on using "I statements" to help me remember how to phrase directions similar to the examples mentioned in the table. Also, the sentence starters "Feel free to" or "You're welcome to" assist me to remain in a Love and Logic mode and assure that I am providing students with implied choices.

Let's take this idea of providing students with choices a step further and define what that looks like. It can feel scary to teachers to be told to share some control in their classroom, especially if student behavior is an issue. We tend to hold on for dear life as it relates to control when working with challenging students. However, strategically relinquishing control is just what needs to happen to remedy poor behavior. This strategy also has the potential to greatly reduce power struggles between teachers and students.

Sharing control involves giving students as many choices as possible throughout a school day. However, teachers must provide choices within limits that are acceptable and manageable to them.

We give control on our terms, or the kids will take it on theirs.

—JIM FAY

The following are examples of choices teachers can give to students that do not negatively impact the learning environment and provide students with opportunities to make some of their own decisions, thus buying back some control in their lives, and with this control, the students also gain skills that assist them to solve their own problems. We all know how well power-hungry students respond to demands. Not at all! Giving choices rather than directives fosters healthy relationships, lessens power struggles, and gives students autonomy over their behavior.

Examples of Choices:

- Would you like to sit or stand while you work?
- Would you prefer to walk in the front or the back of the line?
- Are you going to do that assignment in pencil or pen?
- Would you prefer to work alone or with a partner?
- Would you prefer to start the assignment now or right after a drink of water?
- Would you prefer to work with the lights on or dimmed, music or no music?
- Or, as I like to ask my husband at the end of the workday, would you like to pour me a glass of wine now or three seconds ago?

With Love and Logic, there is a shift in thinking to what we expect students to do rather than warn them about what they can't do and then punish them should they choose to go to the dark side. Providing choices within our own boundaries is a simple shift that will make a tremendous difference in classroom climate. There are guidelines for effectively implementing the strategy of choice in the classroom. They are as follows:

1. Choices must be legitimate. Do not give a choice that is obviously sarcastic or not doable. For example, "Are you going to finish the project now or at the turn of the next century?" Use of sarcasm will incite a power struggle and take a very effective strategy and make it highly ineffective.
2. The choices must be acceptable to the teacher. Teachers should never provide a choice to students that they do not want the student to select because we all know what will

happen; they will choose the adult's unpopular choice. For example, "Would you like to sit in the office for a few minutes or until the end of the day?" Sitting in the office all day is actually fun. Students people watch and get out of doing their work all day. Don't provide choices that will sabotage the effectiveness of this behavior strategy.

3. Offer choices with equal emphasis. If teachers emphasize the choice, they prefer the student to select; the savvy student will pick up on this hint and often choose the opposite choice just to engage in a power struggle.

There is an art to providing choices. The following sentence starters assist me in providing choices to students effectively.

"You're welcome to _____ or _____."

"Feel free to _____ or _____."

"Would you rather _____ or _____?"

"What would work best for you _____ or _____?"

> A first-grade teacher stands in the doorway of my office with one of her frequent flyers to the office at her side. She says, "He is up to seventy-eight laps around the playground due to his disrespectful behavior." I say, "That will be great exercise for him. I will be happy to walk with him and give you a break." She huffs off, and I lace up my tennies for a punishment that might take the entire day or week to complete.

Love and Logic provides educators with rules and consequences in order to avoid situations like this where a punishment is unreasonable and undoable and pits the teacher and the student against one another. However, no matter what we do as educators, students will break the rules, and we must have a solid plan in place that addresses the problem while teaching the students how to make better choices. This is done by establishing clear expectations and teaching students to solve their own problems rather than depend on a teacher to do that for them. Let's take a look at what a Love and Logic classroom looks like.

Rules should be established but in a manner that does not lock the teacher into an automated list of consequences. Such systems do not work and force teachers to handle diverse situations with universal strategies. An example of rules in a Love and Logic classroom would not include all these options but would be phrased in the same fashion.

CLASSROOM RULES

- Feel free to do anything that does not cause a problem for anyone else.
- I teach when there are no problems or distractions.
- I listen to students who raise their hands.
- Please treat me with the same respect I treat you.
- If someone causes a problem, I will do something.
- What I do will depend on what happened and what the person is willing to do to solve the problem.
- I allow students in our classroom as long as they do not cause a problem for themselves or anyone else.
- If they cause a problem, I will ask them to fix it.
- If they can't or will not fix it, I will do something.
- What I do depends on the unique situation.

Do you notice how these rules communicate what is expected rather than what is not expected as it relates to behavior? As Jim Fay believes, "Rules are based on principles rather than symptoms." This is a powerful shift in thinking and creates a classroom climate that is based on respect and shared control. Rules stated in this format do not lock a teacher into handling every situation with the same reaction or consequence.

The word *fair* often comes into play when dealing with student discipline. Get over it! Life is simply not fair; however, teachers must handle disciplinary situations with equity by assessing the situation individually, giving students opportunities to solve the problem themselves while providing guidance and assistance as needed, and here is how to make that happen.

CONSEQUENCES

The effective teacher administers consequences with empathy and understanding as opposed to anger and lecture.

Kids will respond positively to a consequence when they see a logical connection between their behavior and what happens to them as a result of that behavior.

— JIM FAY

The first Love and Logic rule of thumb as it relates to delving out consequences is that they do not have to be delivered immediately. Although it is best to resolve a situation in a timely fashion, it is not always best practice to do so. Educators often feel pressured to have an immediate solution to every behavioral problem. When feeling pressured, teachers often do not make the best decisions. Feel free to take a bit of time to reflect on the situation prior to rendering a consequence. Jim Fay calls this technique the "Delayed Consequence," and

I have found it to be one of the greatest assets to resolving conflict. When used, the teacher should communicate to the student that this is a unique situation and one that requires some thought. Phrases such as "I am not sure exactly how I want to respond to this situation. I will think about it and get back to you when I have some options in mind" not only buy the teacher or administrator time but are much more effective, in that all parties have time to calm down and think more rationally. I have even used this with parents when I have had to reach out to them to discuss their child's behavior. I assert that I want to be fair, and in order to do so, I need some time to reflect, call a colleague, check our policies, or run ideas past my supervisors or law enforcement before rendering a decision. I have also sought input from parents by asking them what they believe would be an appropriate consequence for their child's behavior. Oftentimes, their recommendations are more stringent than I would have recommended.

Next up is the delivery style of said consequence. Remember, in a Love and Logic classroom, the student is involved in the problem-solving process in order to not only teach them how to solve problems but also give them the confidence in knowing that they can solve their own problems. Their self-esteem grows from such experiences as do their grit and determination to resolve future altercations. When a problematic behavior occurs, utilize the following guidelines to share the ownership of the problem with the student and teach them how to solve their own problem while at the same time preserving the relationship with the student even during trying times and situations.

1. *Empathy:* As educators, we sincerely care about our students, and when they misbehave, we need to demonstrate that love and caring by interacting with them with empathy. Although we might be frustrated or angry with them regarding their behaviors, we cannot let that show. We must begin an interac-

tion after any behavioral infraction with empathy, not anger. Sentence starters include "I am sad that _____."; "How sad that _____."; "I am sure it feels awful when _____."; and "Oh no, I'll bet that makes you unhappy when _____." Empathy communicates to the student that the teacher cares and is sincerely saddened by the misbehavior. Empathy rather than anger or frustration is a powerful tool.

2. *Power Message:* The interaction between the educator and the student continues with what Jim Fay coins as a "Power Message." A question like "What are you going to do about _____?" or a statement like "I'd like to hear your ideas of how you could solve this problem" is extremely effective and places the decision-making power with the student, which is right where it needs to be.

3. *Pose Questions and Consider Choices:* When working through a behavior situation, it is critical that the student do the majority of the thinking in order to gain competence in this skill. The following are sentence starters to get a student thinking about how to resolve a situation:

   - "What would you like to have happen?"
   - "Is it possible that _____?"
   - "How do you feel about _____?"
   - "Is there any chance that _____?"
   - "How do you suppose that might work out for you?"
   - "On a scale of one to ten, how good of a decision do you think that is?"
   - "If you cannot think of any solutions, would you like to know how other students have resolved similar situations?"

These sorts of questions force students to think and problem solve at high levels, thus building their skills in this critical area for success. If the student does not have any ideas as to how to resolve the situation, the educator can step in and give the student choices.

4. *Assess Consequences:* As ideas to resolve a problem are discussed, the educator must provide reflection opportunities to the student by asking the question, "How will that solution work for you?" or "Will that solution work for everyone?" If the answer is no, back to the drawing board. Providing time for such reflection models for the student how problems are resolved authentically.

5. *Bid Them Well:* The problem-solving process concludes when the educator affirms to the student that a decision has been agreed upon and wishes the student the best of luck for success. This message must be delivered with sincerity without any sarcasm to be effective. "I bet it will feel good when this situation is resolved, good luck!"

It is critical that the adult remains calm during all interactions revolving around student behavior, which can be challenging when emotions run high. Take a step back, delay the consequence, and do whatever is necessary to assure healthy interactions between the educator and the student.

Maintaining a Love and Logic classroom benefits both the teacher and the students. Relationships remain intact due to a system that is built upon the principles of trust, respect, and shared control. Students are doing the majority of the thinking, thus taking much of the decision-making responsibility off of the teachers' plates. Power struggles diminish due to the strategy of providing students with questions and choices about their behavior and consequences, thus empowering them with a sense of control over their lives at school, and down the road, in the workforce as adults.

BEHAVIOR DATA POINTS

- Student Risk Screening Scale: Internalizing and Externalizing (SRSS-IE, Ci3T)
- Fastbridge
- Special Education Referrals and Individualized Education Program (IEP) Progress Reports
- Attendance
- Tardies
- Office Discipline Referrals
- In-School and Out-of-School Suspensions
- Visits to the Nurse
- Participation in School Activities

I return to my classroom after being gone for a medical appointment to find the substitute seated at my desk, feet up, newspaper in hand, earphones blaring, and a smoldering cigar dangling from his mouth! My students have moved the classroom furniture to the back of the room and are competing in their own version of Grade School Olympics. Well, not my original lesson plans, but at least they are getting their physical fitness in for the day!

Of course students' physical health is critical for their success in school, especially if they are in training for the Grade School Olympics, but their emotional health is an area where teachers have had little time and training and are asked to deal with daily. Educators need skills in their arsenal to address the emotional well-being of their students in an effort to assure not only students' mental health but the mental health of themselves as well. Take a deep breath; inhale and exhale, in preparation for chapter 5.

FITNESS CHALLENGE

1. What is your vision of an ideal classroom?
2. Select and read one of the books listed in this chapter in an effort to improve classroom management skills.
3. Design a positive reward system for your classroom utilizing either a ticket or an electronic point system.
4. Visit and review the Love and Logic website at www.love-andlogic.com.

CHAPTER 5

THE ABCs OF SURVIVAL

THE CHARACTER OR SOCIAL-EMOTIONAL DOMAIN

One of my students has escaped from the school building and is running about the football field putting on quite the show. Teachers are chasing him and asking him nicely to return to the school to no avail. I am called to assist. I take my resource officer with me in an effort to "motivate" my student to return to the building. When we arrive on the scene, he immediately drops his act. He walks over to the track that encircles the football field, stretches out on the ground face down, puts his hands behind his back, and says, "Cuff me, Officer!"

This is the domain that is unchartered by most educators. Students are coming to school today with far greater emotional needs, such as a student who runs from the school requiring teachers to chase him and ultimately knows the drill for being arrested. Reasons for such behavior could be the effects of poverty, the pandemic, compromised mental health, trauma, or other complex factors unknown to the school staff. The bottom line is that educators must be equipped to address the emotional needs and well-being of the students they serve.

According to Dr. Lane and her team, there are five areas for social and emotional learning:

- Self-Awareness
- Self-Management
- Responsible Decision-Making
- Relationship Skills
- Social Awareness

The team also identified the top ten social-emotional behaviors critical for student success:

- Listen to Others
- Follow Directions
- Follow Classroom Rules
- Ignore Peer Distractions
- Ask for Help
- Take Turns in Conversations
- Cooperate with Others
- Control Temper in Conflict Situations
- Act Responsibly with Others
- Show Kindness to Others

Teachers used to count on school counselors to be responsible for instruction in this domain, but this is no longer the reality. Too many students come to school daily without these skills in place; hence, they must be taught. I can already feel your anxiety level escalating, and I get it. I am here to tell you that you are already dealing with students who struggle to regulate their own emotions, make responsible decisions, and have the capacity to maintain healthy relationships with adults and peers. You just need a framework to navigate these situations more seamlessly, and that framework is at your fingertips.

Teachers must be equipped with a social-emotional curriculum that is research based and validated. This curriculum must be taught with fidelity and implemented by every classroom teacher. Once taught and reinforced, students will begin to acquire healthier social-emotional skills, which will ultimately lead to fewer conduct issues and greater academic gains.

SOCIAL-EMOTIONAL CURRICULUM AND STRATEGIES

IES WWC: What Works Clearinghouse: This is a site that reviews curriculum and offers research-backed recommendations. If a school district does not have a social-emotional curriculum, this is a great starting place to research which program might be the best fit for your school.

- Second Step
- Character Strong
- Zones of Regulation
- MindUp
- Olweus Class Meetings That Matter
- Character Development and Leadership (Secondary Curriculum)

- Mindfulness

Interestingly, there are a number of data points that can be telling about a student's emotional health. There are two fundamental areas of concern to note: Internalizing Behaviors and Externalizing Behaviors. These behaviors should be assessed three times a year, and there are a variety of assessments that have a social-emotional screener. It is critical to identify students who are suffering in order to implement interventions in a timely fashion. There are multiple data points to assess students' emotional well-being such as visits to the nurse's office, absences/tardies, discipline referrals, bullying referrals, special education referrals, counselor and social worker visits or referrals, and whether or not a student participates in school activities. Such data points tell a story about the overall health of a child and provide critical information to educators.

SOCIAL-EMOTIONAL SCREENERS OR ASSESSMENTS

- Student Risk Screening Scale: Internalizing and Externalizing (SRSS-IE, Ci3T)
- Fastbridge

GROWTH MINDSET

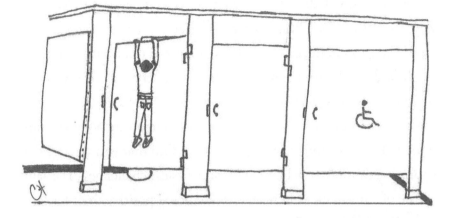

The custodian comes to my classroom to inform me there is a problem with the boys' restroom. I look around my sixth-grade classroom and note a few worried eyes. He continues to tell me that the stall doors have been torn off their hinges every day for a week. I tell him that I am certain I can resolve this issue. We have a class meeting where I learn that my boys have been doing what they call a "Shaq Attack" on the bathroom doors. I give them a perplexed look not knowing what they mean. They explain that a "Shaq Attack" is when they pretend to dunk a basketball on the bathroom door and hang on the "Rim" in celebration of a great shot. I explain that those doors are expensive to replace even for a pro basketball player. Game over!

So often, the chatter in our brain, or our self-talk, is negative, which creates unhealthy habits and limits our opportunities. We need to teach our current students to think like the boys in my class who were preparing to become NBA players. There are no limitations as long as we don't set them upon ourselves, and there are educational strategies to implement to teach such skills to our students.

In the research done by Carol Dweck regarding Growth Mindset, she asserts that your brain is a muscle, and it has the potential to grow, change, and learn new skills and habits! If our brain is a muscle, think back to the time when you decided to try that new workout program as we discussed earlier. The first time you went, the routine was rigorous and exhausting. The next day, your entire body was sore, but you kept returning to the gym only to find that you were getting stronger and more capable to take on physical challenges. The same is true of your brain. You must exercise being positive in order to be more *fit* emotionally. That being said, have you ever gotten into shape and then fallen off the wagon for even a few days? What was the result? It was like you were starting the fitness regimen from scratch! You must stick with this mental exercise program in order for the results to be long-lasting.

In *The Growth Mindset Coach*, the authors offer a great analogy to describe thinking habits. Since we are comparing teaching to survivor reality shows, we will picture ourselves on an island rather than the forest they describe. On this island, each day, you take the same path through the rainforest to the beach. You have created a walkway for yourself where the ground has settled into a path, there are no branches, and rocks or weeds blocking your way, thus making your travels carefree. However, if you decide to create a new path to the beach through the rainforest, then you have to work far harder because you must clear the path of debris in order to reach your destination. Your brain works the same way. Your old habits of mind are easier to employ because you have created well-defined paths in your brain. Transitioning to a new mindset will not happen overnight. You are going to have to clear the debris from the path, but it is possible. It will take time and concerted effort to create this new road map of thinking!

A first-grade teacher calls the office for administrative assistance. I make my way to her class and find that the student in question is actually seated outside of her room. I ask about the problem only to learn that this child has refused to do his work, is hissing at other students, and claims to be a snake. Sensing that this teacher needs a break from this young man, I ask him to accompany me to my office. He does. However, he opts to slither all the way to the office, making the commute a bit longer than intended. I take my time and enjoy the slow, scenic route.

This student took on the challenge of creating a new pathway to the office, which was both creative and admirable. Adopting new thinking habits is a powerful way to increase the health of not only the students but for you as well.

A Fixed Mindset Says:

You can eat that piece of candy.

A Growth Mindset Says:

I bet you can't eat the entire bag.

CHALLENGE ACCEPTED

THE GROWTH MINDSET COACH, ANNIE BROCK, HEATHER HUNDLEY

The work of Carol Dweck and, subsequently, the authors of *The Growth Mindset Coach*, Annie Brock and Heather Hundley, outline a powerful approach of working with children and adults. Their approach asks us to consider the notion that people tend to look at the challenges faced in life with either a Fixed or a Growth Mindset.

A person with a Fixed Mindset believes that they are born with an innate set of skills that are fixed and cannot be changed through practice and hard work. A person with a Growth Mindset believes that anything can be learned with purposeful attention and practice. It is critical, as educators, to teach our students to adopt a Growth Mindset.

Teaching the concept of a mindset begins with teaching students that their brain is a muscle, and it can grow and learn new concepts and skills. Comparing the brain to other muscles in the body is a great way to demonstrate the brain's capacity to get in shape! Teachers must also utilize praise and feedback that call attention to a student's perseverance, grit, and effort and avoid praise that calls attention to students' innate talent. Hence, say to a student, "That was an amazing concert you gave on your cello; you must have worked very hard to learn music that is so challenging" rather than "You are one of the most amazing musicians I have ever heard; you are so gifted in music." The first type of praise places the emphasis on the student's effort, whereas the latter focuses on innate talent and skill.

The distinction of this sort of praise is important for a couple of reasons according to Dweck. When we praise students for their innate skills and abilities, it teaches students that they can only thrive in areas of strength that they came by naturally. This sort of praise stifles students, in that they do not think that they can grow in areas that do not come as naturally to them, so they are less likely to try something challenging, new, or difficult. Students also become afraid of looking bad if they make mistakes because they have thrived easily in their areas of strength. They become perfectionists due to the ease they have experienced in accomplishing tasks that come easily to them and are unwilling to try something more difficult for fear of looking stupid or incapable.

Students with a Growth Mindset believe in the power of an important word, *yet*. When they try a new or challenging task and face difficulty, they have been taught that they don't know how to do that skill *yet*, but with practice and dedication, they can learn any new skill. Growth Mindset students are more likely to take risks because they are less afraid of making mistakes. In fact, in a Growth Mindset classroom, mistakes are praised and accepted as a natural part of the learning process, which is such a healthier outlook.

I am supervising the lunchroom when one of my more challenging students comes up and gives me a huge hug. I am touched that she hugged me. I have been working for months to build a positive rapport with this student, and she has been a tough nut to crack. After this student exits the cafeteria, one of the workers approaches and informs me that I have two large tomato soup handprints on the back of my suit jacket. So much for progress.

Well, I may not have made as much progress with this student as I had hoped, but I now believe in the power of the word *yet,* so there is hope on the horizon. Another way to assess the power of the word *yet* has to do with how we assess our students.

GROWTH MINDSET GRADING SYSTEM

I would venture to guess that the majority of today's schools still maintain a traditional grading system that is determined on percentages and grades ranging from an A to an F. It is very difficult to change such a system, but think about how damaging such a system can be to a person's self-esteem. Most likely, students in such settings have also been members of Fixed Mindset classrooms where the "Smart" kids always outperform the other students. The same students' names appear on the honor roll semester after semester. There are a couple of strategies to implement in order to combat this traditional school of thought.

1. Grading System: One idea proposed by Carol Dweck is to assign grades such as an A or a B, but if the student's grade on a project or on a report card is lower than that, assign the student a "Not Yet." This sort of grade allows students to feel as if anything is attainable; they just have not mastered said skill as of yet. Rather than assigning poor grades, which turns students off to learning, assign a grade that empowers them to keep trying.

2. Honor Roll Shift: Take the typical honor roll, and turn it into a Growth Recognition List honoring students who made growth in any measured area. In order to be motivated to learn and persevere at school, students must feel success on

some level. Repeated failures or never making the honor roll is demeaning and depletes motivation.

GRIT

The skill that our children need more than any other skill is grit. You might be thinking that income, intelligence, or test scores are more important than grit, but the truth of the matter is that although all these factors contribute to a person's success, it is grit that takes a child from any background with any level of intelligence to new levels. Hence, we do not discount other factors that influence success, but we do know that having grit without a doubt will contribute to one's growth in any area they desire. We have all worked with extremely bright students who do not have any motivation. They may be intelligent, but they do not have grit. Flip this situation around. A student who struggles in school but has a wonderful work ethic has a much greater chance of attaining their dreams than the highly intelligent child who lacks perseverance and stamina. However, both these types of students would benefit from teachers who recognize effort and structure their classroom around the Growth Mindset qualities.

We must teach our children the importance of grit by praising their effort, acknowledging that mistakes are a part of the learning process and not to be embarrassed of being wrong but celebrate wrongness as a part of the learning process. Failure is just a stepping stone away from success.

Teaching our students that they can learn anything as long as they are willing to make mistakes and put forth effort levels the playing field for all students in a classroom. Everyone can learn and grow as long as they are willing to put forth effort, persevere, and have grit. Teachers who integrate the power of the word *yet* in their classrooms teach students that learning is a process, not an event. There is a great deal of power in the tiny word *yet*.

Relationships come in all shapes and sizes, but there is one thing for certain that students do not learn from teachers they feel do not like them or from teachers they do not like themselves. The role relationships play in a school setting is one of the most powerful roles that fosters not only academic achievement but social and emotional well-being as well, even if some students show their love by leaving tomato soup imprints on your heart or your clothing.

TEACHER–STUDENT RELATIONSHIPS

One cannot emphasize enough the importance of teachers fostering healthy relationships with students. A healthy relationship is a result of trust, kindness, and the belief that the teacher sincerely cares about students and believes that they can succeed. Students learn from teachers they care about and who care about them in return. When redirection or critique is needed, teachers focus less on the student and more on the approach or process the student used that did not work for them. Criticism is not personal; mistakes are a part of the process.

INSTRUCTIONAL CHALLENGE

A Growth Mindset classroom promotes the concept of learning over mastery of a concept. Mastery is the bonus that comes with grit and perseverance during the learning process. Teachers challenge students at high levels and praise students' effort while they work. Students are encouraged to take risks, and mistakes are a valued aspect of the learning process. Students are presented with a variety of instructional strategies and choices, thus tapping into their diverse learning styles.

Assessments: The goal for all students is that they learn. In a Growth Mindset classroom or school, students should have opportunities to retake assessments if they demonstrate that they did not understand a concept. Failing is unhealthy and damages self-esteem. Use the term *not yet*, and allow students to practice and retake assessments when needed. Students learn that understanding or learning about a content area is more important than just a grade.

Training the Brain: Students need to be taught how to regulate their emotions when they are faced with challenges. Rather than giving up or quitting when something gets difficult, they need to know how to step away, take a few deep breaths, and then return to their work. Exercising with students and teaching them yoga and mindfulness routines are wonderful ways to teach students how to tackle their work with vim and vigor, take a break when needed, and then persevere through challenges. These are the skills that are going to make our students successful, not just in school but also in life.

> *I am in the fifth grade and in a classroom where I have a very healthy relationship with my teacher. She is extremely positive and makes me believe I can do anything I want in this world. Out of the blue, I start signing all my assignments with not just my first name, Marcy, but also as "Marcy the Great," with a hand-drawn smiley face visual. I am not sure how long this went on, but one thing I am certain of is that this teacher never asked me to stop, and I now call my positive brain voice, Marcy the Great; move over, Doug!*

Name Your Brain: Self-talk can make or break students. Teachers must integrate instruction around the importance of positive self-talk in an effort to grow stamina and perseverance when tackling challenges. You have learned that my Fixed Mindset name is "Doug." He can be so annoying, but I make efforts to recognize when Doug is antagonizing me and keeping me from achieving my goals. Bringing that self-talk to a conscious level and purposely shifting that line of thinking to the positive is a powerful habit. Move over, Doug; Marcy the Great is back, and she is stronger than ever!

One school year, I had my teachers all wear one of those trendy plastic bracelets. Each time they said something negative to themselves, they had to change the bracelet to the other wrist. We had wonderful discussions about the power of this exercise during faculty meetings. When I feel as if I am trending on the negative, I will often repeat this exercise for a week to get myself back on track.

ATTRIBUTES OF A GROWTH MINDSET CLASSROOM

- With practice, effort, perseverance, stamina, and grit, anything can be learned, and a child's potential is limitless.
- The brain is a muscle and can grow and become better fit just like any other muscle in the body. Students are taught how the brain functions.
- Mistakes are a part of the learning process and should be praised and celebrated.
- Praise is centered around students' effort rather than talent.
- Grades could be based on earning an A, B, or a "Not Yet" status.
- There is a classroom theme centered around Growth Mindset, and Growth Mindset Language is common.
- All types of student work are on display, including work that highlights mistakes.

- Maintaining a Growth Mindset is a part of the classroom rules.
- Parents of students have been taught how the classroom will incorporate the tenets of Growth Mindset.
- The classroom grades revolve more around learning than mastery. Goals are set about learning content rather than mastering facts for a test.
- Exercise, yoga, and mindfulness practices are integrated regularly.
- The teacher has established healthy relationships with the students. The students trust the teacher and are willing to take academic risks because they are not fearful of being wrong or making mistakes.
- Students are challenged with a variety of instructional strategies as well as instructional choices.
- Phrases like "Give it a whirl" or "It's worth trying" are used to encourage students to persevere and work hard.

MINDFULNESS

Mindfulness is a powerful practice that many of our students have had little or no exposure to in our classrooms. Integrating mindfulness into classroom routines teaches students to regulate and manage their own emotions. It assists them in learning how to respond to a world that is chalked full of stressors. For some reason, our current lifestyle has us overscheduling, working long hours, and never allowing ourselves to simply savor the moment. It is critical for ourselves and our students that we change this habit, and it starts in our classrooms.

Mindfulness is a practice that is over twenty-five hundred years old and has become popular again in the past few decades but not necessarily in classrooms. When I first implemented mindfulness at my school, I received a couple of phone calls from families concerned that I was promoting religion. Although mindfulness does have religious roots, the purpose for using the practice in schools is to teach students how to focus, regulate their emotions, and build resiliency.

Mindfulness asks its practitioners to live in the present moment with an awareness of thoughts and emotions without being judgmental. The practice of mindfulness allows us to observe and accept thoughts as they come and go without reacting to them with emotion. Mindfulness can be as easy as taking a slow breath in through your nose and blowing it out through your mouth or an extended period of time in a quiet location seated in a particular manner without distraction. Even taking a pause several times a day to take a few extended breaths is beneficial and will improve one's ability to cope with the stressors of teaching and school.

There are many benefits for teachers and students with the integration of mindfulness into the school setting such as the following:

- Increase in attention and focus
- More on task behavior
- Teachers and students learn to regulate their own emotions
- Decrease in student behaviors and decrease in anger and aggression
- Ability to regulate emotions
- Decrease in task avoidance
- Increase in compassion and empathy for others
- Decrease in selfish behavior
- Reduced stress
- Increased awareness of self and others
- Increase in academic achievement
- Mental health improvements

- Decrease in interpersonal problems
- Decrease in anxiety and depression
- Decrease in burnout and feelings of hopelessness about work
- Reduction in test anxiety for students

The good news is that you can change your brain from the stressful ball of anxiety to one that is far more relaxed and able to tackle the anxiety of any day in a more calm and thoughtful manner. Practicing mindfulness in schools is even more critical in that children's brains are just developing. Teaching ways to handle stress and regulate their emotions at a young age will help them to develop healthy problem-solving skills when they are adults and forced to navigate the real world. They will have the strategies to avoid knee-jerk reactions to problems and rather learn self-awareness and strategies to regulate their emotions so that they can have thoughtful reactions during stressful interactions.

Both students and teachers can benefit from the daily integration of mindfulness into the school setting. It is exciting to think that such a simple practice for even a few minutes a day has the potential for such a positive and powerful impact on students and teachers.

The following are ways to integrate mindfulness into a school setting:

- Deep Breathing: Simply have teachers and students take several deep breaths in through their nose, hold their breath to the count of five, and blow their breath out through their mouths.
- Heartbeat Activity: Have students take their resting heart rate for a minute and record it. Then, have them do jumping jacks or run in place for a minute and check their heart rate again.

This activity helps students develop an awareness of how their body feels at rest and how it feels when it exercises.

- The Five Senses Activity: Take your class for a walk or remain in your classroom while asking students to notice one thing that they see, hear, smell, touch, and taste, in an effort to make them more aware of what their body is experiencing concerning their immediate environment. If taste throws them for a loop, provide a snack for the activity or ask them to describe what the air tastes like.

- Take a Mindful Walk: Ask the students to pay attention to their feet. What their feet felt like as they walked. They should only concentrate on their feet in an effort to teach them to learn about their own bodies. When you return to the classroom, share their experiences as a class.

- Have a Mindful Leader for an elementary classroom just like a Line Leader. They can choose a morning mindfulness activity and lead the class in the exercise.

- Have students keep a mindfulness journal where they record how they feel each morning when they arrive at school. You can have them record entries before and after mindful activities in an effort to show them how much better they feel when practicing mindfulness.

- Make a Mindfulness Glitter Jar: With a water bottle, clear liquid glue, and glitter, students can create a mindfulness jar. Once made, they can shake the bottle and watch the glitter settle, which resembles how with mindfulness, the brain can settle down just like the glitter does in the bottle.

- Hot Cocoa or Pinwheel Breathing Exercise: Have students pretend they are holding a hot cup of cocoa or purchase small pinwheels for students. Have the students take long deep breaths in and exhale with long breaths to cool their cocoa or spin their pinwheel. Have them then take short, quick breaths both in and out with the same exercise and then compare how both types of breathing made them feel.

- Tense and Release: Have students practice tensing a certain set of muscles, such as their arms, and then releasing the tension, noting the difference in feelings.

- Square Breathing: Have your students close their eyes and envision a square. Have them take a breath in while they trace their imaginary square in their mind. One side of the square represents a breath in, whereas the next side of the square will represent an exhale. Students continue to trace the square with their fingers while breathing in and out.

- Coloring is a relaxing and wonderful way to integrate mindfulness. Google mindful coloring pages for kids, and your resources are limitless. Students will enjoy coloring while they learn from the messages on the coloring pages.

- As a class, watch the movie *Inside Out*, and discuss the main character and her emotions. Compare her emotions to their own life experiences with their own emotions.
- Integrate short yoga lessons into the daily routine.

- Provide students with a mindfulness BINGO card for the week. Provide incentives to earn a BINGO! A HyperDoc could also be used so that electronic options could be provided to students for mindfulness choices.

- Play the "What would you do?" game with students. Have situations printed on strips of paper. Take a few moments to pull a strip, and read the situation to the class, such as "One of your friends asks you to be mean to a classmate." What would you do? Students then share their responses and listen and learn how others would handle the same situation.

- Read a book to students about mindfulness, and discuss as a group the content from the book.

- Listening Exercise: Go to various locations, and have students close their eyes and listen for a short period of time. Discuss what it was that they heard when they chose to only focus on listening.

- Lead students in a guided meditation. The following are six free applications available to students and teachers.

    1. <u>Calm</u>
    2. <u>Headspace</u>
    3. <u>MyLife Meditation</u>
    4. <u>Smiling Mind</u>
    5. <u>Dreamykid</u>
    6. <u>Insight Timer</u>

- *Mindfulness Monday:* Every Monday morning, I teach the staff and students a new mindfulness activity over the intercom. The teachers are then charged with practicing this activity at the start of each day the remainder of the week. Transition times are great opportunities to practice mindfulness activities. Coming back in from recess, right before taking a quiz, and at the start of a new lesson are all great times to take a moment and regulate both your students and your emotions. Yes, you should model and practice these activities with your students. Such activities do not have to last more than a few moments or be elaborate in structure.

OTHER MINDFULNESS RESOURCES

- Smiling Minds Application
- Headspace Application
- mindfulschools.org
- Mindful.org
- heartmindkids.com/how-to-make-a-glitter-jar-for-mindfulness/
- Mindfulnessexercises.com
- simonandschuster.com
- yogajournal.com/teach/tools-for-teachers/
- jbcnschool.edu.in/blog/benefits-of-yoga-in-schools/
- mosaickidsyoga.com/kids-yoga-teaching-resources-tools/
- teachstarter.com/us/blog/tips-teaching-yoga-kids-us/
- weareteachers.com/books-about-mindfulness/
- www.pocketmindfulness.com/best-mindfulness-books-for-kids/

- imaginationsoup.net/mindfulness-books-kids/
- readbrightly.com/mindfulness-meditation-books-for-kids/
- mindfulmazing.com/15-mindfulness-books-for-kids/
- weareteachers.com/teacher-guided-meditations/
- mindfulnessexercises.com/
  building-confidence-for-social-settings/

TEACHER SOCIAL-EMOTIONAL HEALTH

A student who is taking a break from the normal routine in order to de-escalate from an impressive meltdown is seated at a desk in my office. He is not ready to have a conversation about what took place. I tell him to sit tight, take some deep breaths, and when his voice sounds like mine, we will discuss the situation. I take advantage of a few minutes of peace when I suddenly hear an odd sound. I look over to find the student eating the lunch I had left untouched on my desk. You snooze, you lose!

If you let your guard down, even for just a moment of peace, you may miss something important, such as your lunch. In order to keep our guards up, we must take care of our own social-emotional health. For years, I have not taken a nonworking lunch. It is critical that we take time away during the day to recharge our batteries in order to be effective teachers. You have my permission to not only take but also enjoy a duty-free lunch. You and I both need it!

EFFECTIVE CLASSROOM MANAGEMENT IMPACTS TEACHERS' MOOD AND BEHAVIOR

Teacher behavior is equally as important, if not more important than, student behavior. There are some tips to take care of yourself behaviorally from our old pal Dr. Sprick and the text, *CHAMPS*.

- When students misbehave chronically, it is easy to fall into the habit of lowering one's expectations. Do not fall into this trap. Maintain high expectations for yourself and your students, and the odds of reaching them greatly improve.
- Take an inventory of your thinking patterns as it relates to your students. Are you unintentionally labeling students in a way that creates negative emotions toward them, such as "They are from a rough family; there is no hope for them."
- Examine your own personal biases. All of us do not want to believe that we have any biases, but our brains automatically categorize information from our personal experiences and from what we have learned. Be aware of your biases so that they do not get in your way professionally even if unintentionally.
- Always maintain a vision of what success looks like for you and your students.

- Do not take student behavior personally. We invest in our students, so it is a natural tendency to be hurt when they betray us with horrific behavior. The bottom line is that this behavior is not personal; do not make it that way so that you can objectively help students to improve.

- Invest in relationships with students. Get to know them. Show them that you care for them. Many of our students have been let down by most all adults in their lives, and earning their trust is a process, not an event.

- *Stay calm.* Do not argue with students. Your own emotions are at risk if you engage in arguments, which is a fast track to burnout. Remain neutral as much as possible in tense situations. Fall back on simple phrases, or do not talk at all until the student is ready to interact with you.

- Create and sustain a positive behavior management system in your classroom. When you look for positive behaviors, it makes you happier as well.

RELAX, ALREADY!

The Back to School Bash is in full swing, and the 5K Color Run is about to start. I enjoy the run while walking with staff and students. After returning to the school, the chief of police pulls into the parking lot. I panic thinking that someone has been hit by a car or has had a medical emergency. No need to panic. The chief was upset because the cheerleaders, who were spraying the rainbow of colors on people as they ran the race, also chose to spray the outline of penises with the color spray on multiple sidewalks in

> *front of businesses along the route. I tell him that art can come in a variety of shapes, sizes, and colors but that we will clean up the carnage immediately!*

The emotional and physical health of our teachers is integral to the success of students. The happier and healthier our staff are, the more likely they are to remain in the profession. Offering our staff both physical and social-emotional opportunities is an essential element to the climate and culture of today's schools, even if it involves a Color Run where the cheerleaders paint inappropriate body parts in front of local businesses.

THE BIGGEST LOSER

At least once a year, I lead my staff in not just a Biggest Loser or weight loss challenge but also an overall health challenge. Typically, I start this effort right after the new year. The challenge is three tiered: weight loss, exercise, and emotional self-care. Teachers can choose to participate in all or just the parts of the challenge that they wish to join. Some examples of prizes for the challenge are as follows:

- Greatest percentage of weight loss. We have a male and female category.
- Greatest loss in inches.
- Trying a new form of physical fitness.
- Greatest amount of exercise.
- Trying a new hobby.
- Taking purposeful time for yourself (going to a movie, reading a fun book, traveling).
- Mindfulness.

- Best new healthy recipe.
- Provide fitness classes in the school gym. There are always teachers who do yoga, Jazzercise, Zumba, or some other form of fitness and are willing to provide free classes to staff members during this challenge.
- Check with local fitness centers to see if they would provide a free or reduced trial offer for teachers during the challenge period.
- Host a staff volleyball or basketball tournament. Students can attend and watch and cheer for the athletes. Celebrate with trophies or medals for everyone.

We have short, weekly gatherings to share ideas and progress or have everyone bring a healthy dish to share. We do have the school nurse monitor weight progress or, in a small district, assign a trusted person to maintain such records.

There are many ways to promote a sense of wellness at school as well. Here are a few of the ideas I have used in my schools to take care of the social-emotional well-being of my staff:

- I purchased rocking chairs for the teacher work room. Not only did they enjoy a calm break, but more people also came to the work room to socialize while they sat and rocked for a few moments.
- Keep an ongoing puzzle out on a table in the teachers' workroom. A puzzle is a great way to take a break from reality and concentrate on something that is manageable. When the puzzle is complete, have a staff celebration.
- TGI Wednesday: Choose a day other than Friday to provide treats for the staff. Every day is a blessing.

- Hire a massage chair to have in the teachers' workroom for a day or two, and have teachers and all other staff sign up for a ten-minute massage.
- Take a traveling cart around the school with a variety of treats. Have each teacher and staff member select a treat from the "Food Truck," so to say.
- Hire a Food Truck, and provide lunch or a frozen treat for all staff and students if it is financially feasible.
- Rent a blowup bouncy house or maze not just for the students but also for the staff to enjoy at the end of the day once the kids have finished playing on it. It is fun to be a kid again!
- Hire a stand-up comedian for a staff meeting or professional development. Laughter is the best medicine.
- Select a grade level or department each Friday, and purchase their favorite fountain drink.
- Host a Pajama Day just for the teachers.
- Purchase a fun book for all staff as a gift.
- Design and purchase T-shirts for teachers and/or students as a way to promote the school community.
- Have the Food Service staff make a special meal for teachers.
- Provide coverage for a teacher, and let them leave an hour early.
- Have a weekly "Superior Staff Member" parking spot, and rotate the recipients.
- Enjoy a dress down day.

Driving to and from Work Applications: Make coming and going from work purposeful, especially if you have any sort of commute. Download applications that can assist you in remembering how to find joy in each and every day. Obviously, you cannot practice mindfulness while you are driving, but you can learn about techniques through audible books or podcasts. Listen to music that is soothing or makes you feel energized and happy. Commuting to and from work provides time to set the stage for the day as well as draw the curtain. Make sure that these moments are spent purposefully rather than just noise on the radio.

Avoid the News: Many of us listen to the news on the way to and from work. There is research to support that this practice is not recommended. The majority of news stories are tragic and even frightening. Think about the news channels during the pandemic; there was a running tabulation of the number of deaths from COVID-19 scrolling across the screen each and every day. For many, this sort of reminder was frightening and not the best way to start or finish your day. Find positive applications or audible books to listen to rather than the news, and you may find that your mindset becomes healthier.

A New You: Whenever I need a "pick-me-up," I will often purchase a new perfume, shampoo, deodorant, or even a new type or shade of makeup to spice things up a bit and feel refreshed. Also, nothing is better than a new haircut and color to brighten one's mood and feel rejuvenated.

Vacation Every Day: Display pictures from your favorite vacations and family or personal moments, not only at home but also, more importantly, at work. My desk and personal bulletin board are filled with pictures of my favorite people and places in an effort to remind me of all the blessings in my life.

Spa Day: When I travel, I have found that I always like the scent of the hotel's shampoo, shower gel, and conditioner. In an effort to be reminded of the wonderful days away from work, I order my favorite scents from hotels we have visited and use them at home, especially on Mondays! I even called the Marriott that we once visited in Florida because the lobby smelled so good. As it turns out, it was an aromatherapy they sold in their spa. I now have that same scent in my family room and office, and I sincerely enjoy walking into those areas and being bombarded with my favorite vacation spot!

Massage: Although life can be expensive, it is critical that you treat yourself to an occasional treat, such as a massage, manicure, or pedicure. I belong to a massage group that offers a discount if you sign up for a monthly massage, thus making it more affordable as well as assuring that I do this for myself regularly.

Coffee House: Purchasing a coffee from a formal coffee house each day can become a financial burden and can be laden with unhealthy calories. Purchase a Keurig along with coffee, tea, and hot chocolate pods to have in your office or desk area. Add in some tasty creamers, and you are set for a delicious indulgence at work where you can control the calories and have a special treat any time of the day.

Deep Breaths: Set a timer on your phone for an hourly reminder to stop and take a few deep breaths in through your nose and out through your mouth. Even this small effort to integrate mindful breathing has shown to make a tremendous difference in stress levels. Even when teaching, it is possible to stop and take a deep breath between lessons or even as you walk about monitoring student progress.

Sugar-Free Treats: This may sound silly, but do *not* let the stress of your job derail you from being healthy and taking care of yourself. I often find myself saying, "I deserve chocolate or chips due to the stress I am enduring at work." *No*; you deserve to take care of yourself no matter the stress level of your job. Keep sugar-free gum, candies, sodas, or other treats on hand when stress creeps into your day. I also keep healthy snack options handy, but sometimes, you need to feel as if you are treating yourself to something special or to an indulgence in the middle of a stressful workday.

Exercise: There are many days when I cannot get to the gym, such as today when I have a PTO meeting and then a Board of Education meeting. Instead of telling myself that I cannot exercise today, I find ways to integrate it into my day. For example, every time I use the restroom, I do twenty squats. I pack tennis shoes so that I can walk in between school and a school event that I have to supervise during the evening. I keep makeup, deodorant, and a hair dryer at school to spruce up between exercise and my responsibilities. By doing this, I do not fall into the trap of saying that I do not have time to exercise. I find thirty minutes that I would have spent in my office at my computer trying to get caught up, which will never happen, and prioritize myself.

Stroll down Memory Lane: This may sound silly, but when I am extremely tense, I enjoy watching some of my favorite television shows from years ago. Nothing perks me up better than an episode of *I Love Lucy, Mash, The Mary Tyler Moore Show, The Dick Van Dyke Show,* or *The Carol Burnett Show.* If you have never seen or heard of these shows, you must look them up; it will be worth your time. These shows remind me of easier times and provide opportunities to laugh out loud, which is exactly what the doctor, Dr. Cassidy, ordered.

Reconnect with an Old Friend: When we are extremely busy, we often let valuable friendships fade into the sunset. We tell ourselves that we do not have time for friends when, in fact, we must invest in such friendships as a way to connect with people outside of the work walls. There really is a world out there; you just have to take the time to prioritize you and your friendships and sneak away for a bit to enjoy it.

It's the first day of Spirit Week and Pajama Day, one of my personal favorites due to comfort! I am conducting walk-through observations when I enter a fifth-grade classroom and stop in my tracks. The teacher is most certainly wearing pajamas. Unfortunately, they might be more appropriate in a honeymoon suite, an exotic chemise and negligee. Perhaps I was not clear enough on the expectations for the actual type of pajamas staff should wear on such a day?

We all know the importance of cultivating healthy relationships with our students, but equally important are our relationships with our colleagues, both professionally and personally, even those with more exciting night lives than our own!

I am working at my desk when an employee comes in and asks to talk to me. I wave her in, and she begins the conversation about how her knee has been bothering her. I ask if she injured it at work, and she assures me that this was not the case. She continues describing her symptoms and then asks for medical advice. It dawns on me that I recently earned my doctoral degree, and staff and students have begun calling me Dr. Cassidy, just not that kind of doctor! Awkward!

Teaching is an isolating profession as it relates to adult relationships. We retreat to our own classrooms at the start of the day, work with students from one period to the next, and if we interact with adults, it takes a concerted effort to do so. Without purposeful collaboration, teachers can be out of touch with the needs of their colleagues and their students, kind of like asking a Doctor of Education for medical advice. However, there is nothing more powerful than the relationships one can cultivate with colleagues. You need them not only as a professional resource but as an emotional resource as well. Administrators and teachers must take purposeful steps to provide staff with such opportunities, or they will be missed.

Late Start or Early Release: Typically, a school district sets aside four to five days for professional learning opportunities for the entire year. Although we take what we can get, this is simply not enough time together to accomplish the goal of professional learning but also to come together as friends and colleagues. One idea that would add more time like this together is to either have students report late or release early to and from school once a week, once a month, or a predetermined number of times during a school year. One concern about this idea is that parents will be inconvenienced. In order to avoid that issue, my school has a late start every Wednesday, but we offer childcare for the families that are in need of such a service. We utilize our paraprofessional and high school students to oversee the kiddos who need to be at school. Another idea would be to rotate grade levels on such days and have staff members not participating that day supervise students.

Professional Learning Communities: The company Solution Tree offers educators formal training for how to best implement the practices of Professional Learning Communities (PLCs); however, such training can be quite costly. Hence, there are numerous books and publications about PLCs from the very same company that can assist school leaders with this effort. PLCs provide grade levels or departments dedicated time to meet weekly in order to discuss four key principles:

1. What is it we expect students to learn?
2. How will we know if they learned it?
3. How will we respond when they do not learn it?

4. How will we respond when they exceed expectations?

Although the conversations around the table are professional rather than social, time is still dedicated for teams to come together as a group and interact about student growth. It is also a time to share professional ideas, review student data, and bond as teams. It is a win-win for teachers and students.

FACULTY MEETINGS

Although it takes effort on the administrator's part, it is critical for entire faculties to come together as a family at least twice a month, if not weekly. As stated earlier, teaching is an isolating profession; efforts must be made to keep lines of communication open as well as to come together for both professional and social reasons. At each staff meeting, take a few minutes to do a team-building activity where teachers have opportunities to have fun and get to know one another better. Such activities allow people to see what they have in common and get to know one another better. In order to have time for such opportunities, assure all housekeeping announcements are done via email or included in weekly announcements or newsletters. Providing breakfast or snacks at such meetings is a nice touch. People will enjoy socializing prior to the start of the meeting. Dedicate time at the front end of the meeting for socialization and the rest for information or professional training, but come together regularly.

TEAM-BUILDING IDEAS

Brain Teasers or Riddles: Have staff members get into partners or groups and solve a fun brain teaser or riddle at the start of a staff meeting.

Professional or Personal Accomplishment: Have teachers write a personal or professional accomplishment on a sticky note. They then find a partner and share what they wrote. They give their sticky note to their partner and find a new partner. They continue to share what was shared with them with a few more people. Finally, gather in a large circle and have a few people share what is on the last sticky note they acquired, and celebrate together as a group.

Compliment Page: Tape an 8½-by-11-inch sheet of paper on the backs of each staff member. The staff is charged with writing something they admire or like about each person on their sheet of paper. They do not have to sign their name. At the end of the activity, teachers can read the compliments their colleagues assigned to them. I have had staff members save their compliment pages for years and take them out and read them on a rainy day as a pick-me-up, so to say.

Show and Tell: Teachers have had their students take part in this ritual for years. Ask a few teachers to share something meaningful or sentimental to them at the start of a staff meeting in an effort to get to know each other better.

Board Game or Team Game: Have the staff take time to play a team game or play a board game instead of hosting a meeting.

Favorite Recipe: Host a breakfast or lunch, and ask teachers to bring their favorite dish along with copies of the recipe to share. Teachers learn about each other as well as enjoy a meal together. This is fun to do on workdays or professional learning days when there is more time to interact and enjoy one another.

Acting Out: Have teachers get into assigned groups and role play student behaviors. The staff can then discuss how they would handle or discipline students when they behave in such a manner.

Pick a Penny: Gather a collection of pennies, and at a staff meeting, have each teacher select one penny. They must see what year the penny was made and tell something about themselves from that year. Have teachers select a new penny if they get one from a year before they were born.

Book Club: Each year, I lead a professional book study, but it is also invigorating to have a monthly book club that reads for fun. Assign a teacher to select the monthly book and gather to read and discuss the contents of the book.

Picture Scavenger Hunt: Assign teachers to a small group or partner. The teachers then have to complete a scavenger hunt where they receive clues for mystery locations where they have to go and take selfies. The scavenger hunt can take place in the school, outside of the school, and off the property if time allows. The teams of teachers return to the school with the selfies as evidence that they have completed the scavenger hunt.

Word Challenge: The principal or administrator creates a list of words around a theme, such as summer vacation. Each word is written on a notecard and then taped to the back of a staff member. The staff pairs up and gives one another three clues as to what the word is without saying the word. The partner must guess what word is taped to their back. They get three guesses, and if they guess the correct word, they sit down. If they have not guessed their word, they find a new partner for three more clues.

Cover of a Magazine: Have teachers create a cover of a magazine in which they would be featured. Have them share their final products highlighting why they would be magazine cover worthy.

Two Truths and a Lie: Each teacher writes two truths and one lie about themselves on a notecard. One by one, they share the three statements, and the staff must guess which of the three clues is the lie.

Rock, Paper, Scissors: Although this is an old game, it is such fun to play. Have everyone find a partner and play three rounds of

Rock, Paper, Scissors. The person who wins two of the three rounds advances, and the other person is out of the game. Keep playing until there are two people left for the championship round, and have everyone watch and cheer!

Walk-Up Song: Just like baseball players, have teachers select their "Walk-Up Song." Play each teacher's song while they strut to the front of the room, and have them share why this is their chosen song as a way to get to know them better.

White Elephant or Garage Sale: Have each teacher bring several items from home that they no longer have a use for and place them on a common table. Teachers are then divided into teams. The teams are asked to take a certain number of items on the table, retreat to their own location, and build something new out of the used items.

> A frustrated teacher arrives at my office with an ornery student in tow. The teacher says, "Tell Dr. Cassidy what you did." The student's response: "Well, I called the bus driver an asshole." Truth telling; he is an asshole.

I often hear teachers lament about how they can handle the problems our children create, but the adult problems are far more stressful for them. Like the bus driver, some adults can simply be assholes, which is far more challenging to deal with, because adults being rude is far more hurtful because it is purposeful. Teachers and administrators need tools to effectively manage the adults in our professional lives. It's too bad we cannot use spiders, snakes, and straitjackets as they do on reality shows for our jobs might be far easier.

I chose to research how to effectively hire teachers as it relates to their interpersonal skills for my dissertation, because in three decades in the field of education, I have found that it is very difficult to help someone change their interpersonal skills even when it would benefit them tremendously. Most of the time, they do not see their negative personality traits as a hindrance, which is part of the problem. Hence, I decided that I need to hire people with competent interpersonal skills to begin with in order to avoid this problem. Take a look at the interview instrument you utilize. Does it tease out information about interpersonal skills? If not, find one that does.

I do have several tips that I have collected over the years and offer to teachers who struggle with their interpersonal skills.

- Own your mistakes, and make efforts to learn from them moving forward. Don't lament over them, fix them, and always strive to be the best person you can be.
- One of the best lessons I learned from my father is you can be right or you can be *dead right* in any sort of disagreement. Teaching is a service profession. We are constantly dealing with the public. Oftentimes, my staff will get defensive when a parent accuses them of making a mistake from something as simple as a grade the parents disagree with, the loss of an assignment, or being angry because the parent feels as if the teacher treated them rudely as a few examples. No matter what, I *always* tell the patron that I did not intend to upset them and that I feel badly that our relationship is compromised. Instead of insisting that I am right, and many times I am in the right, I take the high road and apologize to avoid ruining our relationship and be *dead right.* I tell my staff that sometimes it is best to preserve the relationship by eating crow and that crow is a rather tasty little bird. Don't be *dead right!*
- Personality Tests: Sometimes it is helpful for members of a staff to take part in personality tests so that colleagues can

develop a better understanding of why people behave the way they do. A couple of the personality tests I have done with my teachers over the years are the Personality Compass and the Color Personality Test. After the teachers learn their compass or direction and/or their color, it is fun to group them in common or uncommon groups during professional development activities. Understanding our personalities and the personalities of others helps us to interact with all people. For instance, in one position, I worked with a colleague who was a last-minute person and a procrastinator. I'm a planner, and I soon realized that I needed to remind this individual of projects, important presentations, meetings, and deadlines. Doing this kept me focused on the job and not frustrated by our personality differences. It also kept the individual more accountable so that we didn't end up in the position where I was having to do their work at the last minute.

- Teachers must be trained to have courageous conversations. As a principal and superintendent, I often have teachers stop by my office and voice concern about a parent or a colleague. When I ask if they have brought the concern to them, the answer is almost always "No." On top of that, they do not want me to tell the other person that they voiced a concern about them. Now, tell me, how in the world is that going to solve the problem? Although such meetings can be stressful, they are necessary if one wishes to truly resolve the problem. Call the meeting, be kind in your approach, and begin the process of repairing whatever is wrong.

- Accept that no matter the problem, you are a part of it in some way, shape, or form. Self-reflection is a skill that takes maturity as well as honesty. We often want to believe that nobody ever talks about us behind our backs or thinks poorly of us. This is not true. Educators work with too many groups of people and engage in social interactions every day of their working career. You will be pushed to your limits, and you will make mistakes. When problems arise, take the time to sincerely assess your part in it, and it will resolve more effectively and efficiently.

- Make a conscious effort to not be a part of the problem but a part of the solution. If you find yourself in a group of complaining colleagues, have the courage to tell them that you are going to opt to be positive this year and will not take part in any negative talk and gossip. Always take the high road. You will be amazed at how much better you feel when you do not associate yourself with the Negative Nellies of your school.

A student is waiting in my office to discuss his latest behavioral concern. I walk in, and on cue, he places his hand on his chest and begins to moan. He then stands and begins staggering about the *office. He concludes the show by twirling around, collapsing to the floor, and stating that he is having a heart attack. I stand and clap and inform him that the curtain has dropped; show's over. He pops up and returns to his chair. Now, it's time to set the stage for a new plot for this young man.*

Setting the stage for a new school year is key to both the students' and teachers' success, and we are in charge of our story, be it a comedy or a tragedy. Dim the lights, for the next chapter will reveal what it takes to create a showstopping school year.

FITNESS CHALLENGE

1. Consider your own mindset. Do you maintain a Growth or a Fixed Mindset? What about your classroom? As an educator, what can you change in your classroom to shift to a Growth Mindset theme and promote grit, perseverance, and stamina in your students?
2. Research one of your favorite heroes, and learn what obstacles they overcame to attain their goal.
3. What did you want to be when you grew up? Did you attain this goal? If so, why? If not, why?
4. What is your Fixed Mindset brain name? What is your Growth Mindset brain name?
5. What podcasts can you listen to on your way to and from work that will help you reside in the best mindset for the day or evening?

CHAPTER 6

THE ABCs AND D
OF SURVIVAL

PROFESSIONAL DEVELOPMENT

When my children were young, they often accompanied me to concerts and activities at my school. On one particular evening, my youngest son is along for a fifth-grade band concert. This is their first concert during their first year of band instruction. I give my opening remarks for the concert and take my place in the front row next to my son. The band begins to play, and my son's immediate reaction is, "Man, they suck!" He is right. A grandmother seated a few chairs down from us has to leave the room because she is laughing uncontrollably, while I slump down in my chair, hoping not too many others could hear his remark.

The last thing a principal or superintendent wants to hear is that a professional development day was a waste of time or that it "sucked" like a grade school band concert! There are very few days that administrators get to work with and train teachers in a school year, so those days must be well planned, meaningful, and highly engaging. They must build excitement about the profession. It is also critical that teachers have opportunities to learn new strategies to take back to their classrooms to keep both teaching and learning fresh.

As the superintendent of a small, rural school district, I oversee the transportation department. Radios are in my office so that I can maintain communication with my drivers at all times. It is early morning, and one of my drivers radios a message: "I have a kid dressed like Captain Marvel at one of my stops. I don't recognize him and don't think he is one of my regulars." I know of a first-grade student who has been dressing like that for the past few days, so I radio back, "Captain Marvel is ours. Bring him on into school." Expect the unexpected!

Often teachers expect professional development days to be boring and a time when they sit and get information from a speaker. When teachers open their laptops and begin checking email, they have checked out of learning and have created their own agenda for the day. Do not allow this to happen. You do not have to dress like Captain Marvel, although you could if you wanted, and you most likely are a superhero, but you do need to make these days filled with the unexpected. Teachers must be so busy learning that they do not even think to take out their laptops for a distraction.

I am called to a third-grade classroom where a young child is throwing objects about the room. I evacuate all the other students for safety. She continues to turn furniture over, empty hand sanitizer onto the floor, stand on her head, tear papers to shreds, and finally comes to rest atop a storage cabinet. At this point, I make my move to try to reason with her while she is still. She answers my questions by barking like a dog. I let her know I do not understand her responses but am willing to wait. She eventually shimmies down the cabinet, walks over to me, and says, "School is boring!" Show's over!

The first step in providing teachers with pertinent and meaningful professional development is to provide something that they need and want to learn about on the agenda, and it is critical that it is not boring! Teachers and administrators are also charged to be actors for they are on the stage daily delivering instruction. If instruction is not delivered in an interactive and interesting fashion, they just might be hit with flying debris! Survey teachers to assess their learning needs, and your audience will immediately appreciate the fact that their input was considered in the planning process. Genius!

You'll find some examples in Appendix A.

I am on a field trip with my sixth-grade students to see the Nutcracker ballet. None of my students has ever attended the ballet. The show progresses into the scene where the Nutcracker Prince and the King of the Mice are engaged in a fierce battle. Out of the blue, I hear one of my students shout, "Kick him in the nuts!" I look over ready to discipline this student only to see he is on the edge of his seat waiting to see who wins the battle. Not wanting to ruin

> *the show for any more people in the audience, I let it go, sit back,
> and enjoy the conclusion of the performance, as does my class.
> Standing ovation!*

By making a purposeful effort to integrate information, the teachers are wanting to learn into the professional development day, and coupling that with highly engaging strategies, you'll find that teachers are more likely to toss their laptops to the side, sit on the edge of their seats, and enjoy the show, even if it isn't the *Nutcracker* ballet.

SUSTAIN: SET THE STAGE FOR TEACHER RETENTION

> *A colleague and I teach in an urban school district where
> classroom management is a sincere struggle. Mid-day, he appears
> in my doorway holding a box loaded with his belongings. He tells
> me that he is quitting. Right now! I have wide-eyed students in my
> classroom, so this is not the time to talk him off the ledge. I speak
> with him later that day to assure he is all right. He informs me that
> he is great. He is not returning to our school. He even threw his
> lesson plan book out of his car window during his drive home! No
> looking back.*

The last thing any administrator wishes is for a teacher to feel so desperate that he packs up his belongings in the middle of a workday and walks off the job. One way to keep excitement in the profession and retain teachers is to provide the students and staff with an annual theme for the school year. I'm not saying it would have kept this guy, but it will keep everyone engaged. I keep the theme a secret throughout the summer, thus generating excitement for the upcoming school year. Teachers will often pop by my office during the summer months and try to persuade me to divulge the theme to no avail. I wait until late July, build anticipation, and then send the staff a newsletter welcoming them back to the new school year and announcing the annual theme.

I begin the process of selecting an annual theme by identifying a professional book study tied directly to the needs of our teachers and students. I recommend surveying staff regarding areas in which they hope to grow as well as analyzing student data to determine what instructional areas need attention or improvement. Seeking teacher input regarding where they wish to improve is critical for buy-in regarding the annual theme. Students are aware and included in school-wide activities associated with the theme. Tie school celebrations, treats, the weekly newsletter titles, professional development, Halloween costumes, holidays, prizes for students and teachers, and the book study to the theme.

> *Due to significant behaviors, a high school student has been called to the school's conference room with his parents and educators to design a plan of action for improvement. He walks in and asks, "Why are there so many people here?" My principal explains to him that it takes a village to raise a student. The student's response: "Well, f--k your village." This meeting might take longer than intended.*

Themes assist teachers and staff to come together as a community (or village) and encourage all parties to both work and have fun together rather than becoming bored and stagnant in their chosen profession. Boredom and unhappiness is a recipe for teacher attrition. Educators must not only enjoy their work but also enjoy where they work if they are to remain in the profession.

You'll find a list of school-wide themes in Appendix B.

It is a typical, crazy day. A kindergarten student is sent to the office because he is sick, and his parents are to pick him up as soon as possible, which turns out to be a couple of hours. After the secretary realizes how quiet it's been, she looks up from her work and is stunned. The child has taken markers, crayons, glue sticks, scissors, yarn, googly eyes, tape, colored pencils, and any other items he so quietly found in the storage cabinets and redecorated the entire waiting area. The walls, the floor, the desktops, you name it, it is covered. She calls me to the office, and when I arrive, I ask the child, "What have you done?" His reply: "Isn't it beautiful?" He has made his mark!

How do you wish to be remembered as an educator? If a trophy highlighting your contributions to your profession were to be added to the trophy case, how would you be honored? The next chapter will help highlight the possibilities that await you.

FITNESS CHALLENGE

1. Select a theme for the upcoming school year for your classroom or school.

CHAPTER 7

DON'T JUST LEAVE; LEAVE A LEGACY

A teacher and student arrive at my office. The teacher seems anxious and upset. I inquire as to what is wrong, and she says, "Take a look at his face." This child has taken scissors and cut off the majority of his eyebrows, leaving just enough hair to make things interesting. I help her place the call to the child's mother.

In order to survive in today's schools, you must assess how much you have on your proverbial plate and determine how you can rearrange or reduce your responsibilities to best meet your personal needs. You do not need to cut off your eyebrows to alleviate your load, but if you are teetering on the decision of leaving your job, something's gotta give.

Oftentimes, educators feel as if they have to be a martyr and do everything for themselves by themselves. This is no longer possible. You must devote time to identifying what you can delegate, what you can eliminate, and, yes, what can wait until tomorrow.

WHAT YOU NEED TO DO RIGHT NOW

- Set a schedule as to when you will arrive at work and when you will leave, and do *not* let anyone derail you from sticking to this schedule.
- Assure that your work schedule allows for personal and family time, every day.
- Plan to stay late one day a week if you feel it is necessary to keep your head above water but no more than one day a week.
- Tap into parent volunteers. Allow them to take on any sort of work that does not breach confidentiality.
- Plan a midweek personal or family fun night. Do not wait for the weekend to do what you enjoy. Go out to dinner, or take in a movie smack dab in the middle of the week.
- Reach out to colleagues for advice, support, and ideas. Do not reinvent the wheel. Share ideas or even share in the planning process in order to divide and conquer as well as save time.
- Identify what you are doing that is *not* necessary. Is there an easier way to write lesson plans? Which assignments must be fully graded and recorded, and which can just be checked

for effort or completion? You cannot grade and record every assignment.

- Meet with your administrator, and get a feel for the professional expectations at your school. Oftentimes, we set the bar higher than it needs to be in an effort to please or impress the principal. Of course, pleasing the principal is important, but get a true idea of what they expect and communicate regularly so that you feel comfortable with your personal level of effort.

- Plan in advance, and always have the materials you need for instruction. Be ready for every lesson, every day. Nothing is more exhausting than teaching on the fly. When you are prepared, you feel better. When lessons are executed well, you enjoy your job more.

- Ask for help! It is all right to ask for assistance from administrators and colleagues when you're feeling overwhelmed. You would do the same for your colleagues as well. Do not struggle in silence. Reach out, and you will be amazed at the level of support you will find. We are all in this together.

- Utilize strategies that actively engage students in the learning process so that they are doing more of the work than you are.

- Utilize a positive and proactive classroom management system or school-wide theme in an effort to create a healthy culture and climate in your classroom or school.

- Engage *only* in conversations that are positive and productive. Excuse yourself from conversations that turn toward the dark side. Tell a toxic person that you have made a promise to yourself to be positive. Then, turn and walk away, *quickly*!

> *A day care teacher at our school often takes the children on walks to visit classrooms and older students. On one of her walks, she stops and buys herself a soda from the vending machine. Upon returning to the classroom, this tiny child announces to the entire group, "We got the beer!" Perhaps, he has heard this before!*

So, you may not be in the habit of drinking beer at school, but what habits do you exhibit that are a detriment to not only your professional performance but to your health as well? I recently read *Atomic Habits*, by James Clear, an amazing book that defines how habits, both good and bad, are formed and then offers practical strategies to make small changes in your habitual behaviors that will result in change for the good. I highly recommend this book. As a matter of fact, I have both the hardcover version and the audible books so that I can review it as often as I need to keep me on track in making choices that form into healthy habits. It is very easy to slip back into old habits, so you must keep these skills on the conscious level.

If you are late to work every day, there are steps you can take to alleviate this problem. Is your classroom management system ineffective? This can also be fixed. Do you struggle to have materials ready at the start of the week or the start of each class? You can do something about this! Oftentimes, there are easy steps to take to eliminate problems that generate a great deal of daily stress. We may not even realize that these habits are contributing to our unhappiness, but they are, and we can fix them with a little effort and commitment to change for the better.

THE MOST DESTRUCTIVE HABIT

However, there is one chronic, habitual problem in schools that is the mother lode of all bad habits, and that is negativity. I see so many educators struggle with negativity daily, and this includes negative self-talk as well as negative talk about the profession. A constant loop of how awful the profession has become and how you cannot take it anymore is a huge downer day in, day out.

Negativity is toxic and makes each precious day you are given a total loss. Make a commitment to yourself today to remain positive as it relates to the profession and to your performance and belief system. If you have succumbed and turned into a negative or toxic individual, there is hope! You can change these behaviors. And once you make the effort to change, you will also feel better. Make your habit to enjoy the moment, celebrate what goes well, and be a positive influence on those around you. You can do this!

A kindergarten teacher arrives at my office with a student in tow. She says, "He refuses to write his name correctly. His name is Cayden, and he signs everything as XYN." I look at the student and ask why he is signing his name with such an interesting grouping of letters, and he leans in close to me and whispers, "Because I am an alien." I think to myself, Dream big, kid!

Every child has a dream, and even if it is to become an alien, it is still a dream. You have a dream, too. It just may be buried under layers and years of stress. It is time to dig it up, dust it off, and make a difference rather than leave the profession. Think back to when you first made the decision to become an educator. Identify the tenets of the profession that spoke to you. For me, I absolutely adored children and wanted to work with them in an effort to assist them in achieving their goals. I found joy in lifting them up, nurturing them, and then, most important, stepping back and watching them flourish. Job well done!

YOUR LEGACY

Ask yourself this: "What is the legacy I wish to leave to my profession? What do I want colleagues and students to remember about the difference I made as an educator?" Defining your legacy gives you a purpose to remain in the profession. It breathes life back into your soul and is a constant reminder of why you do what you do.

> I am working one-on-one with a student who struggles with behavior. Out of the blue, he grabs my glasses off of my face, puts them on, and begins to run around the room. At first, I am alarmed, but then I realize that my prescription is so significant that this child surely cannot see where he is going or what he is doing. Sure enough, within seconds, he brings my glasses back to me and says, "These do not work."

It is time to take a close look at what your legacy is going to be, with the correct lenses and prescriptions, of course. In order to begin thinking about your own legacy, I will share what I have designed for myself.

My legacy is twofold. First of all, after thirty-four years in education, I have been seated around a conference room table more times than I can count to discuss a student's Individual Education Plan (IEP). At each meeting, educators and support staff discuss where the student needs to improve. There have been students who I have worked with throughout their entire educational journey, and to be honest, their growth or improvement was minimal at best. Why is this? I believe that this is because school districts are required to assess students who struggle academically and then design interventions that will assist the student to improve in said areas of deficit. The problem with this overall prescription is that we are concentrating only on our students' weakest academic, behavioral, or social-emotional points. Although all students need fundamental reading and math competencies in order to thrive in school and in the real world, and we absolutely should build around such deficits, we should also draft goals around the students' strengths. I am not a chemical engineer for a reason. The skills needed for such a profession are not in my wheelhouse at all, nor are they my strong suit or even my interest. I believe that the world of special education needs a wake-up call. If we are going to help students who struggle in school, we must not only concentrate on where their weaknesses lie but also identify their strengths and add goals to their educational plans that strengthen areas where they thrive and, ultimately, may have a professional interest. If we continue to narrow our focus on students' weakness, we are doing our students a great disservice. We have it all wrong.

IN SEARCH OF STUDENT STRENGTHS

School leaders and teachers must add a battery of assessments or surveys to identify students' strengths and interests. There are a number of options available to educators:

- Myers-Briggs Type Indicator (MBTI) Career Aptitude Test
- Holland Code Career Aptitude Test
- Motivational Appraisal of Personal Potential (MAPP) Career Aptitude Test

- Keirsey Temperament Aptitude Sorter
- The Princeton Review Career Quiz
- Career Explorer Career Test
- My Majors
- The Personal Values Assessment
- iPersonic Career Test
- Work Interest Wizard
- 123 Career Test

I am meeting with a student who has been sent to me because of disruptive and disrespectful behavior. After several rounds of discussions without making much progress, I ask him point blank, "What are we going to do to solve this problem?" His response: "Well, one thing for sure; we cannot re-elect (the current President) to the White House!" We may need more think time.

Putting our political differences aside, when we have the formula wrong for how to best meet students' needs, we are not solving world problems, but we may be contributing to student dropout rates or their complete loss of interest in school. Can you imagine if each day you were forced to work only on the skills in areas of personal deficit? Now, students do have elective classes, but those classes in isolation do not tease out their strengths. Rather, they explore possible interests. We must assess students for such interests and strengths and then align these data points with authentic educational opportunities to build students up and prepare them for a professional future best suited for them.

STUDENT INVOLVEMENT

My legacy also involves inviting interested students to work alongside me to publish this book! These students have gotten a taste of what it takes to tackle one's dream, and I tapped into other students' talents in order to design and create my website. Others assisted in the process of putting together the production of my professional podcast. Creative students handled some of the artwork for my book. It is my hope that I can introduce students to real-life opportunities that will propel them forward professionally. Working alongside students in an effort for them to be inspired to learn and grow while I continue to learn and grow is an important facet of my legacy.

Not only do I hope to leave a legacy as it relates to students, but I also hope to have a lasting impact on you. I have spent years working as an educator in a variety of settings with teachers from all walks of life and stages in their careers. This book is my legacy and hopefully a gift to you. It's a call to action that will give you hope and the skills needed to remain in the profession and leave a legacy all your own rather than leaving the profession altogether due to exhaustion and burnout.

I would love to come to your school and share my professional experiences with other educators who are in this profession to make a difference in the lives of children. Please visit my website at marcycassidyconsulting.com to schedule a visit.

I receive an SOS call from the classroom that services students with significant behaviors. Upon arrival, I discover that furniture and school supplies are airborne. When the student takes a breather, I remind him that we are here to help him and that he might want to think about not continuing this behavior because he will have

> *to clean up his mess and replace anything that he damages. He looks directly at me and says, "You're fired," to which I respond, "Thank you!"*

Having been officially "fired," I will conclude this book with a final thought. You chose education as your career. Now, I'm asking you to choose the tools from this book to rekindle that passion you once had. People in our profession can change and save lives. You need to start by saving your own. You are a valuable asset to each child and family you serve. Our profession is not without its challenges, and I've lived them, believe me. On my website, you'll find stories and inspiration of people just like you. You'll also find tips to help you develop the skills and, just as importantly, the resiliency we all need for the survival reality show that is today's teaching terrain. Let's make this a community of survivors in which no one feels alone and all contestants are inspired to return season after season.

FITNESS CHALLENGE

1. Design and plan the legacy you will leave in the profession of education.

APPENDIX A

PROFESSIONAL DEVELOPMENT ACTIVITIES

Coffee Shop: First of all, stage the learning area as a coffee shop. Provide the teachers with coffee, creamers, and typical treats served in a coffee shop. Just like musicians sing and authors read their work in a coffee shop, teacher leaders can take the stage and share professional development ideas in a similar format. So, provide a microphone. There could be a theme for the day, such as classroom management or how to actively engage students in the learning process, but have the teachers share practical ideas for all to enjoy in a relaxing environment.

Carousel: This activity can be used as a way to start or conclude a day of professional learning. Utilize chart paper by posting pages around the perimeter of the learning environment. Write prompts for teachers to respond to as they rotate around the room as if on a carousel. Each group of teachers must respond to each prompt. At the conclusion of the activity, each group must finish where they began the activity. Then, as a whole group, share what was recorded on each piece of chart paper. Prompts should be centered around a central theme for professional development.

Scavenger Hunts: There are a variety of ways to utilize scavenger hunts during professional development. When utilizing scavenger hunts as a team-building activity, assign teachers to groups and assign them clues to find in various locations, both on and off campus. Perhaps, they could take a selfie at each location as proof of completion. Another way to make learning fun is to use a scavenger hunt to review a professional article, a handbook, or even new curriculum. In teams, teachers have to read through assigned sections of documents and answer questions to the clues provided, thus providing an entertaining way to learn about or review important information. Share responses to the clues as a whole group.

HyperDoc or Menu Learning: It is difficult to cater professional learning to an entire staff who teach a variety of content areas. In an effort to ensure that learning is pertinent to all groups, provide teachers with a menu of learning activities to select from for the day. Such options can be in a written or electronic form. A HyperDoc is like an electronic BINGO card. Links can be included in the boxes, which will broaden learning options. Choice is a powerful tool in engaging learners at all levels, students and adults alike.

Talk Show Host: Although this will sound like a lot of work, it is so much fun. Stage learning in the format of a talk show. We moved a couch and chair into the learning environment to set the stage. A teacher, and there is always one, can serve as the talk show host. They invite the "guests" to their show, and they share their expertise. Teachers can dress in costume, use microphones, sing songs, dance, and even provide prizes to the audience. Make tickets for admission, and have a free concession stand to make the environment even more authentic. Of course, the guests will share meaningful information, and the prizes can even be books for a professional book study, highlighters, sticky notes, or pens, but one thing is guaranteed—the audience will enjoy the show.

Guest Speakers: Let's face it; teachers get tired of hearing from the same people all of the time. Shake things up, and invite a special guest to speak on a topic of interest and need. Consider sharing the cost of a professional speaker with more than one school to make this effort affordable.

Stand-Up Comic: Laughter is the best medicine, and there are many amateur comedians out there who love to come into schools and thank teachers with a funny presentation. Teachers also enjoy a few moments of levity to break up the stress of new learning.

Mindfulness: Always integrate a variety of mindfulness activities during a day of professional development in an effort to model what we expect our teachers to do with our students. These opportunities teach them new techniques to take back to their classrooms. There are many free and easy mindfulness activities to choose from on the web. Tap into these resources, and teach your staff how to regulate their own emotions.

Yoga: Invite a yoga teacher to lead the staff in a relaxation exercise. Modeling the importance of finding ways to relieve stress is certainly an important skill to teach educators and should be included in any day of professional learning.

Art: Invite a local artist or art teacher to lead teachers in an artistic exercise. This will challenge teachers to possibly do something outside of their comfort zone, which is what teachers challenge their students to do each and every day.

Your Other Hand: This exercise asks the participants to read a short story and then draw the main character, including as many of the specific details about the character with their nondominant hand in order to assure that everyone is on a level-playing field. Once participants have finished their drawings, display them one at a time and determine who in the group captured the most details about the main character. This is not only a great activity for adults but also a great activity for teachers to take back to their classrooms.

Exercise: Many educators are so busy that they do not take the time to take care of themselves physically. Invite a PE teacher, local trainer, or physical fitness expert to lead teachers in a physical activity. Spice it up with activities such as Jazzercise, circuit training at a gym, or bowling. The sky's the limit, and perhaps a few of the teachers will find an activity that will help them to become more fit and healthy. These facilities often have rooms they use for parties, so the day could be spent with both physical and traditional learning opportunities. Ask if they will let you use their facility at no charge with the hopes of generating new memberships.

Walk and Talk: Find a route inside or outside of the school, and map out the distance of the route. Pair up teachers, give them a topic to discuss, and send them out to walk and talk. Teams share what they discussed as a whole group upon return from the walk. Teachers can continue to walk on their own and track their distance. Recognize teachers who have tracked their mileage at staff meetings in a way to honor those who have opted to take good care of themselves physically and mentally.

Videos or Movies: There are so many valuable videos and movies at our fingertips, thus allowing us to bring professional speakers right into our schools via a few clicks. Provide a free concession stand with soda, popcorn, and treats, and have teachers enjoy the production. Provide them with prompts or questions to respond to during the video in an effort to keep them engaged as well as topics to discuss at the conclusion of the show.

Tailgate Learning: Have the teachers bring tailgate paraphernalia, such as lawn chairs, coolers, and yard games, to a professional development day. Breaks can involve corn hole, tossing a football, or any other yard game, and lunch can be burgers and hot dogs on a grill provided by the PTO or cafeteria staff. The environment alone will provide a relaxing and fun atmosphere for learning to take place.

Fun and Games: Stage learning activities in the format of a game show with contestants, questions, and answers, or have teachers learn materials in the format of a game. For example, post the answer to a question on the electronic board. One teacher faces the board while their partner faces away. The teacher facing the board must give verbal clues for the other teacher to guess the correct response or utilize an electronic format from a game show, such as Jeopardy, with questions and answers. Music from popular game shows can be used to add to the atmosphere and make learning fun.

Theme Day Learning: Professional development days occur during all seasons. Have the day take on a theme, such as a Halloween Costume Contest, crazy fan day with staff dressed in their favorite team gear, an ornament or cookie exchange, teacher coffee mug exchange, Hawaiian or Summer Vacation Day, and white elephant exchange during learning breaks. The list could go on and on, but a theme for the day always brightens the mood.

All You Can Eat Buffet or Golden Corral Day: Have each member of the leadership team take on a different topic to present during the professional learning day, creating a buffet-like variety of learning opportunities to experience. Teachers will be divided into groups and will rotate through the varying learning options. Lunch could also be a buffet provided by staff members; everyone brings a dish to share. You can also have them bring their favorite dishes with the recipes to share.

Breakout Boxes: Just like breakout rooms, this activity has teachers solve clues to break into toolboxes that are secured with multiple locks. Teachers are divided into teams and given clues needed to open the locks secured on the boxes. These boxes can be purchased or made in-house at a greater discount. How to build the boxes and breakout box lesson plans are available online. Once teachers are able to get all the locks off their box via the clues for the combinations, they find a prize inside the box. There could be an additional prize for the group that breaks out first.

Visit Other Schools/Classrooms: One of the best ways for teachers to learn is to visit and observe other educators. Coordinate with high-performing schools, and spend the day in an authentic setting learning from colleagues. Make sure to have purposeful time upon return to reflect and share ideas that were learned.

Professional Article: Find several pertinent professional articles, copy them, and have teachers break into groups to read and assess the article assigned to them. The teams then create a lesson plan to teach the article to the whole group. Encourage teachers to get creative with their lesson plan, giving colleagues ideas and strategies to take back to their own classrooms.

Book Study: Every school year, lead a professional book study with teachers. Buy the book for the teachers, and provide highlighters and flags that they can use while they read to note critical information.

Make the book study a part of each staff meeting as well as professional development days.

Staff Meetings: Take advantage of each and every staff meeting by providing teachers with one "Golden Instructional Nugget" to take back to their classrooms. It can be tied to a book study, a professional article, a video, an instructional strategy, or classroom management tip. There are so few professional learning days integrated into a school calendar that administrators must take advantage of each and every opportunity the staff comes together as a group to tie in professional learning.

Weekly Announcements: Weekly announcements offer administrators an additional venue to highlight good teaching as well as share a strategy of the week. Look for examples of teachers using the weekly strategies during walk-through observations, and highlight them in pictures in upcoming weekly announcements. Keep learning fresh and in front of teachers in every way possible.

Create a TikTok Video as a Team: Take a professional topic, and have teachers get into groups and create TikTok videos. Share the videos with the entire group, and vote on the best video. Share the videos with the students as well. This is their platform, and they will greatly enjoy and appreciate seeing teachers utilizing modern technology and being silly while they learn.

Student Panel: Invite a panel of students of all ages to describe instructional strategies or projects that have been most meaningful to them. Have them also describe traits of teachers that have appealed the most to them over the years. Avoid using specific names of teachers, and stick to the actual traits that fostered not only relationships but learning as well.

Theater or Acting Out Activities: Invite a local theater buff to lead the staff in impromptu learning activities where teachers have to act out scenarios or respond quickly to verbal prompts. Some will feel intimidated at the start of the festivities, but by the end of the day, they will have laughed while they learned and collected great ideas to use with their students.

Community Tours: Oftentimes, teachers new to the district, and sometimes veteran teachers, are unfamiliar with the community in which they serve. Offer a bus tour of the community, pointing out the highlights, or visit a local museum so that teachers can appreciate and learn about the unique features of their community.

Food Truck: Providing lunch for teachers during professional development is a fun way to keep the teachers together at the school for lunch rather than going out to lunch with their grade level or a couple of close friends on the staff. The food truck will provide them with time to get to know one another better in a casual setting. Inviting local food trucks to the event supports local vendors and adds an element of fun to the day. If necessary, provide teachers with talking topics during lunch as conversation starters. They can use them if they feel the need and can break the ice with groups who do not know each other very well.

Project CRISS: CRISS strategies force teachers and students to interact with any curriculum at a deeper level. Training is necessary, but local teachers can become certified trainers. I highly recommend this training. The strategies are engaging and challenging for both students in classrooms and educators during professional development. Participants of CRISS activities are often asked to transform information from one format to another, thus causing them to think and analyze at higher levels. More information regarding Project CRISS can be found at their website: www.projectcriss.com.

Walk-Through Observations: Tie weekly walk-through observations to whatever topic has been reinforced or identified through both formal and informal professional development opportunities.

APPENDIX B

SCHOOL-WIDE THEMES

HOLLYWOOD THEME

Book Study: The Innovator's Mindset by George Couros or *Teach Like a PIRATE* by Dave Burgess
Weekly Newsletter Title: The Spotlight
Phrases and Words to Use Associated with the Theme:

- Meet Our Cast, Now Showing; In the Spotlight, "Reely" Great Strategies; Now Starring; Set the Stage for Success; Red Carpet Teachers and Students; Lights, Camera, Action; Let Your Personality "Pop" (associating with movie theater popcorn); It's SHOWTIME, Lights, Camera Action (or AUCTION for a fundraiser tied to the theme); Opening Night for an Open House; VIP Hall Pass; Wall of Fame; Red Carpet Event; Casting Call; Awards Night

Activities:

- Welcome teachers and students back to the new school year on an actual Red Carpet. Ask PTO members to act as the paparazzi and take pictures to post on the district website and Facebook pages highlighting the return of teachers to the school community. Have the school mascot dress for the occasion as well to pose for pictures on the Red Carpet.

- Teachers decorate their own Gold Star about their great accomplishments, likes, and personal details for the school's "Walk of Fame." Party supply stores sell gold stars, or they can be found online or made inhouse. Students could also participate in this activity with their teachers. Display the stars in a prominent location for all to admire. Pictures can be taken of "fans" visiting the Walk of Fame and posted on the district's website and Facebook page or even on a school bulletin board.

- Sightings of "famous" local people can be highlighted in weekly announcements, newsletters, and social media pages.

- Have the staff work together to create a YouTube or TikTok video doing a Flash Mob welcoming students back to school or simply highlighting the amazing teachers who work at the school.

- Ask staff members and students, if age appropriate, to send a letter or reach out to their favorite celebrity asking them what strategies they used to become famous or successful in their profession. Staff can write to actors/actresses, authors, athletes, or musicians; the sky's the limit. You will be amazed at how many teachers receive correspondence back from these individuals. Share responses with all staff and students, and post them in a secure location for all to admire.

- Host a movie night for students, staff, and their families. Be mindful of copyright rules that must be in place to show a movie.
- Have a photo booth on site during school events to capture famous moments.
- Host Movie Trivia with prizes.
- The Passing Statue: Find an Oscar-looking statue, and have teachers pass the statue at staff meetings by giving them a compliment, pat on the back, and then the statue. The recipient passes the statue at the next staff meeting.
- Host an Awards Night at the end of the school year.
- Host dress-up days themed after popular or iconic movies.

Prizes:

- Emmy Awards: At staff meetings and professional development, award a bag of M&M's as an "Emmy Award" for a great performance in the classroom. I would use examples of lessons that were noteworthy that were observed during walk-through and formal observations.
- Traveling Trophies: Select weekly challenges, such as attendance for classrooms or classrooms that have made the most growth in an academic area, and have one or more traveling Oscar Awards.
- STAR-shaped notes of encouragement or compliments.
- Starburst candy.
- Star-shaped stress balls or fidgets.
- Place teacher names into movie titles or starring roles on a bulletin board.
- Movie theater tickets and gift cards.
- Frames for their famous pictures.

- Boas in school colors.

Food or Treats:

- Variety of popcorn treats, concession stand treats, Starburst candies, red licorice (red carpet ropes), fancy cupcakes, non-alcoholic drinks for staff served in champagne glasses, Red Carpet (velvet) cake, popcorn balls

CONSTRUCTION CREW THEME

Book Study: Learning by Doing, Richard and Rebecca Dufour
Weekly Newsletter Title: The Weekly Blueprint
Phrases and Words to Use Associated with the Theme:

- Caution ~ Students and Teachers at Work; Strap on your Toolbelt for a New Year; Introducing Members of the Crew; Design Blueprints (lesson plans); Build or Construct Learning; The RIGHT Crew; The RIGHT Tools; Reduce Bad Attitudes to Rubble; Breaking Ground for a New Year; Project or Lesson; What's in YOUR Tool Box?; Dig in for a Great Lesson or Year; "Kid"struction Zone; Dig into a Great Meal; Use Caution Tape and Construction Zone Signs to decorate school; Construction ZONES of Regulation; Work Area Ahead; This Year Will Be LOADS of Fun; FUEL Up for a Great Year

Activities:

- Team-BUILDING Activities.
- Build a Pringles Potato Chip Ring.
- Create and Construct a Staff Puzzle to Display.

- Keep a Puzzle on a Table in the Teacher's Workroom as an ongoing project to promote working together.
- Build or Construct Ice-Cream Sundaes.
- Set up an obstacle course for students and staff to complete.
- Utilize Breakout "Toolboxes" with staff during professional development, and have teachers use them with students in their classroom.
- Play Jenga and Giant Jenga (ask teachers to bring the game from home).
- Traffic Cone Ring Toss with Prizes.
- Have the teachers create something with Play-Doh or kinetic sand.
- Have a buffet for teachers, and ask them to Fuel Up for the year.

Prizes:

- Teaching tools (Fun teacher supplies, such as pens, pencils, desk supplies)
- Hard hats with the school logo
- Bubblegum tape measures for how far you have come or GUM
- Lunch boxes or bags with the school logo so that teachers can eat on the "Site"
- Lunch box foods; individually wrapped items
- Snacks or fuel for teaching
- Energy drinks or Gatorade
- Water bottles with the school logo
- Ball caps or hard hats with the school logo
- Stress or "wrecking" balls in construction tool shapes

Food: (Food can be served in party hard hats and dump trucks)

- Cheese balls, malt balls, or any round candy or treat that resembles a wrecking ball; candy corn or bugle chips (construction cones), build ice-cream sundaes, personal pizzas, baked potato bar, burgers and toppings, orange soda floats, frosted pretzel stick "beams," bubblegum tape measures, mini chocolate donuts (tires), Chex Mix (nuts and bolts), brownies (dirt or mud), decorated individual sugar cookies or cupcakes, crushed Oreos, pudding and gummy worm "Dirt" treats, donut holes as boulders

ENJOY THE RIDE THEME

Book Study: Enjoy the Ride, Steve Gilliland
Weekly Newsletter Title: The Weekly Travel Log
Phrases and Words to Use Associated with the Theme:

- Breaker, Breaker … Get Your Ears On for a Great Year; Keep On Truckin; Roger That (at the end of the newsletter and morning announcements); Start Your Engines; Road Map to Success (mission, vision, values, and goals); Drive Your Career to New Heights; We Are on This Journey Together; You Are Responsible for Reaching Your Destination; Sightseeing New Strategies; Pit Stops (breaks, treats refuel); Road Map to Better Results; Convoy to a New Destination; Beware of Driver Fatigue; Keep On Rolling

Activities:

- Show clips from the movie, *Smokey and the Bandit;* "We've Got a Long Way to Go and a Short Time to Get There."

- Take a driving tour of the school community, and discuss what people knew and did not know about their professional community.
- Encourage teachers to keep a Travel Log or Journal of the School Year, highlighting all the positive things that have happened to them.
- Have teachers make a Bucket List of all the places they wish they could visit and share with others. Have those who have been to some of these places share their memories or photos.
- Have teachers share about their favorite vacations.
- Keep a map of the world in a visible location. Place pins where students and staff have visited.

Prizes:

- Trucker ball caps with school logo.
- Truckers collect pins for their hats; award hat pins to teachers for holidays, birthdays, and special school occasions; pins are available online and in party supply stores.
- Place rocking chairs similar to Cracker Barrel or truck stop for a relaxing break on their pit stops during the school day.
- Toy cars in high-end models for great lessons.
- Road signs with the teachers' names.
- Sodas from favorite fast-food restaurants or gift cards to the restaurants.
- Travel items, pillows, books, and magazines.

Food:

- Food trucks such as ice-cream truck, snow cones, hot dog, and local vendors; cater in from truck stops or Cracker Barrel; travel food favorites; fountain drinks from favorite local spots

THINK PINK

Book Study: Think Pink, Daniel Pink
Weekly Newsletter Title: The Pink Ink
Phrases and Words to Use Associated with the Theme:

- Tickled Pink That you Teach Here; The Pink Elephant in the Room (tease out what needs to be changed); Hot Pink Ideas or Lessons; the color pink represents kindness; provide teachers with pink cardstock cards to write notes of kindness to their colleagues; Look on the Pink Side of Life; Pretty in Pink; Be a Flamingo in a flock of pigeons; Think Pink; Pink Power; Rose Tinted Lenses; The Pink Panther Solves ALL Problems

Activities:

- The color pink represents kindness; provide teachers with pink cardstock to write notes of kindness to their colleagues.
- Flamingos are pink only if they eat a proper diet. Focus on health during the school year with exercise, mindfulness, and nutritious recipes as a way to remain pink in health.
- Invite a yoga or exercise expert to your campus throughout the school year to introduce teachers to new physical fitness options.
- Have teachers log physical fitness hours, and have awards for categories such as most hours logged, new exercise regimen, weight loss, and best healthy recipe.

Prizes:

- Pink highlighters to use with the book study, pink school supplies, pink T-shirts with school logo, flamingo-shaped toys, magnets, pictures, or party favors, pink flowers or plants, pink pig-shaped items, bottles of pink lemonade, and pink water bottles with school logo

Food:

- Bubble gum, pink lemonade, cotton candy, strawberry cake or cupcakes, strawberry floats, strawberry yogurt parfaits, healthy food options (pink in health), such as granola bars, salad bars, sugar-free options, smoothies, pink apples, pink lemonade, pink-frosted animal crackers, "Pig Out" buffet, and strawberry-flavored candies

WHAT'S UP DOK? (WEBB'S DEPTH OF KNOWLEDGE) *LOONEY TUNES* THEME

Book Study: Diving into Strategic Thinking: A Teacher's Field Guide to Depths of Knowledge, Gwendolyn Leininger and Sandra Adams
Weekly Newsletter Title: What's Up DOK?
Phrases and Words Associated with the Theme:
Bugs Bunny Quotes:

- Don't Take Life Too Seriously; You Will Never Get Out Alive.
- Of course I talk to myself, sometimes I need advice from an expert.
- Jumpin' without a parachute? Kind of dangerous, ain't it?
- The way I run this thing, you'd think I knew something about it.

Daffy Duck Quotes:

- I think you're pretty tough, don't I?
- I'm so crazy I don't know this isn't possible.

- Don't shush me. I'll make all the noise I wanna.
- I'm allergic to pain, save me!
- You're Deththpicable!

Pepe Le Pew Quotes:

- I'm "scent" tamentle.
- She must resist me because I am irresistible.
- You are my peanut; I am your brittle.
- Is it possible for me to be too attractive?
- I am playing it too cool, no?

Foghorn Leghorn:

- Looks like the boy genius is trying to show me up.
- Pay attention to me, boy. I'm not just talkin' to hear my head roar.
- Kid don't quit talkin' so much he'll get his tongue sunburned.

Tasmanian Devil Quotes:

- Taz hungry.

Sylvester the Cat Quotes:

- Sufferin Succotash.
- Avoid all people who are negative in their disposition.
- I always stay away from negative individuals because their presence confuses me.
- While chasing my dreams, I fell down and got seriously hurt.
- Boy, you're going to exceed your limits, be careful.
- All cats should meditate from one time to another. If they don't, they will fall in serious trouble.

Tweety Bird Quotes:

- Gosh, I never wealized that being a wittle bird could be so compwicated.

Wile E. Coyote Quotes:

- Genius, that's what it is, sheer genius.
- Being a genius certainly has its advantages.
- A wise decision, my friend. You saved yourself from a fate worse than the frying pan.
- Well, back to the drawing board.

Porky Pig Quotes:

- TH, Th, Th … That's All Folks!

Activities:

- Use a quote from a *Looney Tunes* character in the weekly newsletter. Analyze the quote or compare it to your school.
- Add clips of *Looney Tunes* cartoons into weekly newsletters, staff meetings, and professional development days.
- Teachers *only* or school-wide Pajama Day since that is the attire necessary to watch cartoons.
- Let's Porky Pig Out: Have a buffet lunch.
- It's "Bunny" a great school year celebration.

Prizes:

- *Looney Tunes* stickers, magnets, memorabilia
- Gifts with apples on them, apple key rings, magnets
- Rubber ducks
- Popcorn containers to use while watching cartoons
- Movie theater gift cards

- T-Shirts, mugs, notepads, highlighting *Looney Tunes* characters

Food:

- Food kids eat while watching cartoons such as cereal, cereal bars, or a breakfast bar with a variety of cereals and milk options, carrots or carrot cake, barbecue (pulled Porkie the Pig), chocolate rabbits, Hot Tamales, licorice strips (Dynomite), apples and apple-flavored items to keep the doctor away (DOK), cheese and quakers, orange foods such as Cheetos, Cheeto balls, orange candy slices for unhealthy "carrot" treats

SUPERHERO THEME

Book Study: GRIT: The Power of Passion and Perseverance, Angela Ducksworth
Weekly Newsletter Title: The Daily Planet
Phrases and Words Associated with the Theme:

- News "FLASH"; "Incredible" Opportunities; This looks like a job for a SUPER teacher; I MARVEL at your work; Classroom teachers are our HEROES; Our work is INCREDIBLE; I "WONDER" who is going to be a HERO this year; Unleash the Superhero in you; Teaching is a superpower; Not all superheroes wear capes, some teach; We teach future superheroes; It's a Bird ... It's a Plane ... It's a (school name) Super Teacher; This year is going to be SUPER; Decorate the teacher's workroom as the Bat Cave or create a reading corner as Batman's cave; We are INVINCIBLE; Get CAUGHT UP in a super book (Spider-Man); Have a MARVELous Year; Teachers are here to Save the Day

Prizes for Teachers:

- School-colored capes and masks
- Superhero T-shirts with school logo
- Encouraging messages written on comic book templates
- Superhero magnets or stickers

Activities:

- Have teachers come up with their own superhero name and identify what superpower they would have if they were actually a superhero.
- Show clips of superheroes from movies and cartoons during staff meetings and professional development.

Food:

- Popcorn, Bugles (catwoman claws), Green Jello Cups (Kryptonite), Tootsie Pops, SUPER SOUP Bar, Hero Sandwiches, Coffee Bar (even superheroes need caffeine), breakfast cereal bar (rename cereals to reflect superheroes, such as Captain Marvel Crunch), cocoa Kryptonite, energy bars and drinks, candy bars renamed with superhero theme

FISH PHILOSOPHY

Book Study: FISH, Stephen Lundin
Weekly Newsletter Title: The Catch of the Day
Phrases and Words Associated with the Theme:

- Attitude is everything; Make work a place you want to be; Feel the energy; Attitude affects the quality of life; Make a SPLASH on your state assessments … lessons … on the first day of school, work, etc.; Dive into a great school year; Gone Fish'n for Great Students, Grades, Teachers, etc.; We may all be different fish, but we swim in the same SCHOOL, It's O'FISH'AL; You're the BEST staff ever; Ocean of possibilities; We are anchored in place for a great year; Kindness is a treasure; It's so good to SEA you; SCHOOL of fish; REEL Good Times; The Fishing Hole Reading Corner; Catch of the Day or Week for Student of the week; You are the STAR fish of our school or class

Prizes for Teachers:

- A treasure box in the main office for teachers to select a prize
- Fish-shaped objects
- Gift cards to local seafood spots
- Gift cards to local sports or outdoor shops
- Flavored waters
- Leave work early (Gone Fishin' License)
- A goldfish pet for their classroom
- Prizes placed in a baby pool, where teachers have to fish for them

Activities:

- Host a treasure hunt as a professional development activity.
- Pool party themes for celebrations.
- Have teachers plan how they are going to make their classroom "World Famous" just like the Fish Market in Seattle.
- The fishmongers at the market all have nicknames. Have teachers select a nickname for the school year and describe why they have selected it for themselves.
- Show the iconic video from *FISH*.

- Check out the official FISH website for training and resources: fishphilosophy.com/fish-book/.
- Host a staff campfire.
- Host a Hawaiian Day at school.
- Host a Cookout for Lunch with hot dogs and hamburgers.
- Use Tackle Boxes to Serve Food.
- Have staff design their own Fishing License.
- Share The Tale of the Starfish from the Starfish Foundation: www.thestarfishchange.org/starfish-tale.
- Host a beach party–themed day at school.

Food:

- Swedish fish, gummy fish, worms, sharks, Goldfish crackers, Gone Fish'n Camp Food (hot dogs, hamburgers on the grill, s'mores), root beer floats to help staff stay afloat, sushi bar, flavored waters representing lakes and oceans, submarine sandwiches, peanut butter and jellyfish treats, bait bar with a variety of treats, large pretzel stick (fishing rods) with a variety of dips, red velvet bobber cupcakes, fish and chips: variety of Goldfish flavors and small bags of chips, Starburst (starfish)

HOW FULL IS YOUR BUCKET?

Book Study: How Full Is Your Bucket?, Tom Rath
Book Study for Students: How Full Is Your Bucket?, Mary Reckmeyer
Weekly Newsletter Title: The Weekly Bucket List
Phrases and Words Associated with the Theme:

- Bucket Filler; Bucket Dipper; Kindness Calendar; How Full Is Your Bucket?; "Filling" Good This Year; Buckets of Compliments; Have you filled a bucket today?; It's time to fill a bucket

Prizes for Teachers:

- Notes of praise or compliment cards in the shape of a drop of water
- Bulletin board to display thank you or notes of praise
- Journals to track positive thoughts and experiences
- Dippin' Dots frozen treats
- Beach buckets filled with treats
- Mood rings
- Gift cards to spas to "Fill" good
- Gift cards to restaurants known for comfort or "Fill" good foods
- Stress balls

Activities:

- Have teachers decorate their own buckets and display them in a common location. Have teachers compliment each other by putting written comments into colleagues' buckets.
- Read a bucket filler book to the staff or students.
- Create a Kindness Calendar each month that has daily acts of kindness for students and staff.
- Have staff create a bucket list and track accomplishments on a central bulletin board.
- Tie classroom rules to the book, *How Full Is Your Bucket?*
- Host a beach bucket party day.
- Make a list of foods the staff have never tried, and create a food bucket list. Try items from the list at staff meetings and professional learning days.

- Host gatherings at locations that provide unique opportunities such as axe throwing, painting, or breakout rooms.

Foods:

- Variety of foods with fillings such as donuts, pies, Ding Dongs, Twinkies, potato bar, tacos, sandwich bar, chips or vegetables and dips, high-protein snacks because they are "Filling," soup served with ladles or dippers, Dippin' Dots frozen treats, dips of ice cream, iced sodas in buckets

THE ART AND SCIENCE OF TEACHING

Book Study: The Art and Science of Teaching, Robert Marzano
Weekly Newsletter Title: The Weekly Palate
Phrases and Words Associated with the Theme:

- Find and use quotes from famous artists and scientists; Paint your future; Discover a New Year; This New Learning Will Explode This Year; Formula; Experiment; Periodic Table Groups; Bubble Up Your New School Year; Bubbling with Excitement; Friendships Are Magnetic in Our Class; Experiment with New Ideas; Erupting with Great Ideas; Blasting Off; Beware of Geniuses; The World Is Your Palate; Create Rainbows

Prizes for Teachers:

- Puzzle Books
- Adult Coloring Books and Pencils or Markers; Coloring Pages for Cost Savings
- Tickets to Local Art Galleries or Exhibits
- Local Post Cards Framed

- Beaker Jars and Flavored Water
- Lightbulbs filled with candy
- Slime
- H_2O Bottles
- Popsicle Party (Called Proton Pops)
- Bath Bombs, Bubble Bath, or Shower Gel
- Paint By Number Kits
- Puzzles

Activities:

- Each week learn about and celebrate a famous artist or scientist as a school community.
- Highlight student and staff art.
- Read the book *The Dot* by Peter Reynolds, and create Dot Pictures with the staff and students.
- Host a science and or art fair as a school.
- Keep a variety of jars in the main office. Each month, fill a jar with candy, coins, or some other item. Have students and staff guess how many items are in the jar. At the end of the month, the individual who guesses closest to the exact number wins the jar and the items inside of the jar.
- Create Volcano ice-cream sundaes with a variety of toppings.
- Swap new recipes or formulas.
- Have staff design statues out of Play-Doh.
- Build a dessert or a salad in a jar.
- Build molecules as a staff with marshmallows and skewer sticks; have staff name their molecules.
- Decorate cookies and/or cupcakes in an artistic manner. Host a contest and vote for the most original design.

- Have staff or students draw or copy a picture with their non-dominant hand, and vote for the picture that exhibits the most effort and skill.

Food:

- H_2O, Popsicles (proton pops), ice-cream sundaes with toppings, cake pops on small paint brushes, fruit trays with a variety of fruits presented in a rainbow, frost sugar cookies in a creative manner

CHAMPS

Book Study: CHAMPS, Dr. Randy Sprick
Weekly Newsletter Title: The Weekly Playbook
Phrases and Words Associated with the Theme:

- This year we are going to cross the goal line; GOAT teacher or student of the week; Full-Court Press; Knocked It Out of the Park; Slam Dunk; Pass the Baton; Curveball; Teed Up; Marathon; We are in your corner; Get the ball rolling; Learning is not a spectator sport; Olympic qualities; Kick it out of the park; Goals we have scored; Our playbook for classroom rules; Tackling a brand-new school year; Blitzing math and reading; Reading is our GOAL; Welcome to the TEAM; Play by the rules; Our team pitches in; Check out the fall lineup; Having a ball in third grade; Get in the game; Get your game face on; All-Star Team; We're Number One; Ready: Set: Learn; Hall of Fame

Prizes for Teachers:

- Trophies, ribbons, and medals for recognized areas of strength

- Water bottles
- Stress balls in the shapes of athletic balls
- Gatorade bottles
- Foam number one hands with school logo
- T-shirts with school logo
- Ice-cold sodas
- Host a tailgate during professional development for lunch, including yard games
- Students versus teachers basketball or volleyball tournament

Activities:

- Have teachers and their classes create banners or pennants that represent their class and display them in a prominent location.
- Design classroom jerseys.
- Create classroom team names.
- Have a concession stand as a treat for teachers.
- Host a SOUPER Bowl party with a variety of soup options.
- Ice-cream party with baseball helmet bowls with school logo.
- Dress in favorite team attire.
- Share favorite tailgate recipes.
- Bring tailgate chairs to sit in during professional development.

Food:

- Concession stand items such as candy, popcorn, hot dogs, nachos, pretzels and cheese, bags of peanuts, grill hamburgers and hot dogs for staff

INSIDE OUT THEME

Book Study: The Zones of Regulation, Leah Kuyper and *Explicit Instruction*, Anita L. Archer and Charles A. Hughes[12]

For some of the themes, I include an academic as well as a theme-related book study.

Title of Weekly Announcements: This Week: Inside and Out

Phrases and Words Associated with the Theme:

- Today's Moments Become Tomorrow's Memories; Meet the Little Voices Inside of Our Classroom; Come INSIDE and Bring OUT Your Best; Welcome to Fourth Grade; It Is a JOY to Have You Here; Making Great Memories Both Inside and Out; Amazing Things Happen Here

Prizes for Teachers:

- Have a gumball/candy machines in the teachers' workroom.
- Print images from the movie *Inside Out*, laminate, and make into magnets.
- Candy or candy bar with a variety of colors of candy in the colors of the emotions: red, yellow, purple, green, and blue (Hot Tamales, red hots, licorice, lemon drops, butterscotch drops, yellow Laffy Taffy in multiple colors), Mr. Goodbar, Werther's Candies, Butterfinger, Charleston Chews, Bit-O-Honey, Slow Poke, Chocolate Kisses wrapped in purple, grape Jolly Ranchers, Tootsie Roll Frooties, Dove Candies wrapped in purple, grape-flavored hard candies, Life Savers, green apple candy, Andes Mints, mint-flavored candies, Double-

---

mint gum, Wintergreen Lifesavers, blue cotton candy, blue raspberry candy, Nestle Crunch, AirHeads, Gummi Sharks, Starbursts, M&M's, Skittles, Sour Patch Kids, Runts.

- Gift cards to area spas and fitness shops.
- Water bottles.
- Spa items, such as lotion, bubble bath, and candles.
- Gift cards to bookstores.
- Gift cards to the movies.

Activities:

- Host a candy buffet in the colors of the emotions.
- Donut "Orbs" for breakfast.
- Create their own orb: Purchase clear Christmas Tree ornaments, and have teachers fill them with mementos about themselves. Display the orbs in a common location.
- Host a family movie night with a showing of the movie *Inside Out*. Be certain to follow copyright laws.
- Have a spa day with a masseuse in the teachers' workroom to promote *joy* or to promote good health.
- Host a family 5K walk or run to promote good health both inside and out.
- Teach and practice mindfulness activities with staff and students.
- Host a "Wear Your Clothes Inside-Out" Day.

Food:

Concession stand food, popcorn, candy in the colors of the emotions, cookies or cupcakes frosted in the colors of the emotions

Comfort Foods to Promote Happiness

- Macaroni and cheese
- Baked potato bar
- Soup bar
- Grilled cheese
- Fried chicken and waffles
- Cinnamon rolls
- Donuts (orbs)
- Queso and chips or a nacho bar

Healthy Foods to Promote Internal Health

- Yogurt breakfast bar
- Healthy snacks, such as packets of nuts and dried fruits
- Flavored water
- Provide a salad bar in the cafeteria for staff
- Smoothies
- Healthy muffins
- Granola bars

OUTER SPACE THEME (OUT-OF-THIS-WORLD SCHOOL YEAR)

Book Study: Big Potential, Shawn Achor
Phrases and Words Associated with the Theme:

- The Next Generation; Out of This World; We Boldly Go Where No Other Has Gone Before; Live Long and Prosper; The Trek for a Great School Year or Great Grades; Out-of-This-World Helpers; Reading Is a BLAST; Blasting Off to Learn Math; Control Center; Today's Mission; In a Galaxy, Far, Far Away, Shoot for the Stars; Our Class Rocks; Space Station Reading or Relaxation Corner; A Universe of Possibilities, To Infinity and Beyond; Over the Moon; May the Force Be with You

Activities:

- Shining Star of the Week (Student and Staff).
- Host a "Planet" Pizza Party: Different Toppings Represent Different Planets, such as Pepperoni Pluto, Sausage or Supreme Saturn, and Venus Vegetarian.
- If our school or classroom were a new planet, what would be its attributes? Name the planet.
- Frisbee or Flying Saucer Competition.
- Create Personal Snow Globes.
- Make a Wish on a Star for the School Year.
- Star gazing: Identify favorite movie or television stars, write to them, collect, and share any responses.

Prizes for Teachers:

- Space-themed candy, Food and Gum, Gift Card to Dairy Queen to purchase a Dairy Queen Blast
- Luke Skywalker bottles or flavored water
- Stress balls in the shape of earth, moon, or star
- Moon sand (stress relief)
- "Hans Rolos" (Rolos Candies)
- Yoda Soda (soda or gift card to favorite spots to buy a soda of choice)
- CHEWbacca Gum (packages of chewing gum)
- Starburst candies
- Glow in the Dark items
- Gift cards to out-of-this-world experiences, such as the spa

- Gift card to book store to purchase a book that will take you far, far away
- Gift card to the movies as a getaway from the real-world experience
- Themed Glow in the Dark T-shirts

Food:

- Space-themed candy or food, such as Starbursts, Mars Bar, Milky Way Candy Bars, Moon Pies, Sun Chips, Cosmic Brownies, Bomb Pops, Wookie Cookies (any flavor), Princess Leia Cinnamon Rolls, Chocolate-Dipped Pretzel Light Savers, English Muffin (looks like the surface of the moon) and toppings, "Meateor" Meatballs, Big and Little DIPpers with veggies or chips, Chocolate Donuts or Black Holes, UFO Bagel Bites, Funyons or Saturn Rings, Little Debbie Star Crunch, Cheese Balls or Moon Rocks, Cotton Candy, or Gravity-Free Candy

Printed in the USA
CPSIA information can be obtained
at www.ICGtesting.com
JSHW021506220424
61657JS00001B/1